STREET WARRIORS

STREET
WARRIORS

STREET WARRIORS

Nicholas Davies

Published by John Blake Publishing Ltd,
3 Bramber Court, 2 Bramber Road, London W14 9PB, England

First published by John Blake Publishing in hardback 2001

ISBN 1 90340 2 18 2

British Library Cataloguing-in-Publication Data:
A catalogue record for this book is available from
the British Library.

Typeset by t2

Printed and bound in Great Britain by
Creative Print and Design (Wales), Ebbw Vale, Gwent.

1 3 5 7 9 10 8 6 4 2

Papers used by John Blake Publishing Limited are natural, recyclable products
made from wood grown in sustainable forests. The manufacturing processes con-
form to the environmental regulations of the country of origin.

Dedicated to Nicholas Taft

CONTENTS

For years, real, strong men have battled it out in the ring. Theirs is the truest sport, and they are some of the hardest bastards the world has ever known. These are their stories ...

CHAPTER 1

The first meeting between Britain's two most famous hard men was deathly quiet, but the atmosphere was electric. Both men were tense, on edge, like volcanoes about to explode. Lenny McLean, king of the bare-knuckle prizefighters, and Roy 'Pretty Boy' Shaw did no more than eyeball each other for ten seconds but they never spoke a word.

Throughout that five-minute meeting in the smoke-filled atmosphere of an East London pub, the two men looked straight ahead, not wanting to talk or even acknowledge the other's presence. Their associates did the business.

This was the first time the two hardest men in Britain had ever met, although they had both won fearsome reputations as fierce, tough bastards who lived by violence and dealt out violence to anyone who crossed their paths.

For months, Lenny McLean, the deadliest bare-knuckle fighter in Britain, had been trying to organise a showdown with Roy Shaw, the infamous prize fighter and professional boxer who feared no one.

Roy knew that most people thought him a lunatic, a ruthless bastard who lived by violence both inside and outside the ring. He liked that reputation; it gave him class and earned him respect. There were few with the balls to take him on, either inside or outside the ring.

But the more Lenny McLean heard of this Cockney hard man with the fearsome fists, the more he wanted to meet him face-to-face, either in the ring or, preferably, in some secret location with only bare knuckles as their weapons. But Lenny's mates warned him that 'Pretty Boy' Shaw was no push-over. He was, in fact, the number-one man in London, a right maniac, the one they called 'The Guv'nor' whom everyone feared.

Every time Lenny heard that Roy Shaw was the self-proclaimed Guv'nor, the more determined he became that they must meet face-to-face to decide who really should have the title of London's number-one prizefighter.

Lenny wanted Shaw's title more than anything.

Lenny had made enquiries, many enquiries. He wanted to know everything about the man who was so feared and so dangerous that grown men thought him a lunatic, a man who would destroy his opponent with his bare fists and then walk away without even bothering to look back.

Everyone Lenny spoke to told him to forget challenging Roy Shaw. Lenny hated that; it made him look inferior and he wanted to be top dog.

Lenny knew that he was the best bare-knuckle prizefighter in Britain by a long stretch. Many had challenged him and he had fought dozens of wannabes but he had smashed every one of them to pulp. After many of those fights, Lenny had left the field of battle with the poor challenger still lying on the ground, the blood pouring from his nose and mouth; his eyes so puffed and bruised the man could hardly see.

But Lenny's respect for the man they called 'Pretty Boy' gradually increased. Lenny discovered that Roy Shaw's profession was violence, the brutal destruction of any man who dared to challenge him.

He learned that Roy was a true villain, a courageous gangster who had been in and out of prison most of his life, mainly for crimes involving violence. He had spent a total of 24 years behind bars, keeping fit, pumping his muscles in gruelling dedication to building his strength. Inside every jail, the name of Roy Shaw brought nothing but respect. Both the screws and the villains knew they should never think of crossing Pretty Boy, otherwise he might explode in a mayhem of violence leaving them at death's door. No one wanted that.

Lenny also learned of Shawsey's extraordinary boxing career in the legitimate boxing world where he had to fight under Queensberry rules. He found out that Roy's career was awesome – ten professional fights, ten victories, six of them knock-outs. There had been few men in the serious world of British boxing who could claim that he had won every major fight he had ever fought. But Roy Shaw could. His trainer/manager Micky Duff was proud of him, convinced that he was the hardest man he had ever trained.

Eventually, after several months, Lenny approached an old mate, Roy Nash, who promoted the odd boxing match, and asked him to fix a fight with Roy Shaw.

'He's a maniac,' Nash warned his mate, 'and he's a hard bastard, bloody hard. Do you really want to take him on?'

'Yeah, definitely,' replied Lenny. 'I have to; it's a matter of honour. I want his title and the only way to get it is to fight him. I'd prefer to fight outside the ring, bare knuckles only, but if he wants a fight in the ring, I'll be happy to oblige.'

'Are you sure?' asked Nash. 'Because this bastard means business. I've seen him fight and he's like a wild animal. I've seen his own corner having to pull him off an opponent who dared to land a few good punches on him. The poor bastard ended up in hospital.'

But Lenny wouldn't be put off. He was determined to take on Shaw and smash him, to prove that he was the toughest bastard in Britain.

'Don't worry about me,' said Lenny. 'I've never yet met a man who can stay upright with me for more than a couple of minutes. You know, Roy, because you've seen me. When I hit someone hard, they never get up, never.'

Roy Nash agreed to try and put a fight together. He warned Lenny, saying, 'It might be more difficult than you think. Pretty Boy decides who he will fight, no one else. People want to fight him just because he is the number one, even if they know they're going to get a fucking pasting. Men drink out free for months after taking a battering from Pretty Boy, because a man who survives a few rounds against him is considered a courageous bastard.'

For a few weeks nothing happened, but Roy had heard of the challenge. He decided to let Lenny sit and stew for a while before agreeing to a fight. Roy Shaw was certain that he would always beat a prize-fighter, even a top bare-knuckle fighter, because he knew from experience that bare-knuckle fighters had no stamina.

Eventually, Roy Shaw let it be known through mates in the East End that he would agree to a fight with Lenny any time. A meeting was arranged in the Green Man.

Roy Shaw walked into the Hoxton pub in London's East End with Joey Pyle, the archetypal gangster respected far and wide by everyone in the London underworld and the fight game. A mean-looking Roy Shaw walked in with him and sat down without saying a word. He didn't even glance at the massive figure of 18-stone Lenny sitting quietly in a chair.

Lenny said later, 'Roy never said a word. He was like a volcano ready to erupt. He didn't look like he was with us; he just stared into the distance, a man in his own world with those piercing fucking eyes.'

Lenny told Joey Pyle he would put three grand into the pot and Joey agreed to match it. The winner would take everything. Joey stood up and briefly shook hands with Lenny McLean, turned, looked at Roy Shaw and walked out. Without saying a word or even looking at Lenny McLean, Shaw got to his feet and followed Joe Pyle out of the pub. That was the end of the long-awaited meeting. It was over in seconds – no introductions, no chit-chat, no drinks, no bull-shit.

Later, Lenny wrote, 'Now, I don't want to give the impression that Roy Shaw is some sort of mental case. I don't suppose he's any nuttier than I am. But he had a way about him where he sort of shut himself off ... saw and heard only what he wanted to see and hear.'

From that moment, Lenny McLean wanted to know all he could about Roy Shaw, the man he knew was a hard-case who could handle himself really well. During their brief meeting, Lenny noted that Roy Shaw was superbly fit and incredibly strong. He would be no push-over.

Lenny McLean and some mates went to the Ilford Palais to watch Shawey in his next fight against a haystack of a bloke weighing 18 stone with a big black beard called Lew 'Wild Thing' Yates. This was a fight everyone wanted to see; 1,500 people had driven from all over London and there were touts making small fortunes on the tickets. All the front rows were taken up by villains and well-known faces.

Lenny described the fight, writing, 'When Shaw jumps into the ring, he looks like some midget by the side of the caveman Yates. From the first bell, Shaw goes at him like a Rottweiler and puts him on his knees. Yates stays there until a count of nine and then gets to his feet. In the second round, he wakes up a bit and gives Roy some lovely belts to the head. There's 18 stone behind those fists, yet Roy never once backed up. Only a few seconds into the third round and Roy tears into the beard and rips up his face. Yates is finished. He's down on one knee, leaning against the bottom rope and his blood's pumping everywhere.'

But the fight had got to Lenny, steamed him up, made him fighting mad. He wanted to fight Roy Shaw there and then. So he leapt to his feet and pulled himself over the ropes into the ring, ready to take on Shawey.

'Let me at him, let me get to him,' Lenny was shouting and screaming. The fight fans that night knew Lenny McLean well; there were few men with the sheer size and weight of Lenny. There was uproar in the audience as the crowd realised it seemed another, unscheduled fight was to take place with a bare-knuckled Lenny McLean taking on Roy Shaw who was still wearing the gloves. They anticipated another fight, one which they were screaming to see.

But Shaw's corner wanted to know nothing of an impromptu fight between the two men, whatever happened. Four of Shaw's heavies quickly surrounded McLean and pushed him away from their man. In fact, a jubilant Shaw had hardly noticed that McLean had jumped into the ring; he was too busy enjoying his moment of victory against the haystack.

Joey Pyle stepped in to control the situation, fearful that an angry Lenny might take a swipe at Roy. That was the last thing he wanted. He knew that would end in fucking murder. It would take ten men to separate them and they would probably get a few broken noses in the process. So Joey grabbed Lenny by the arm, desperate to calm him, speaking quietly to him, saying, 'OK, Lenny, that's enough ... leave it out ... you've got your challenge but not tonight.'

Lenny tried to shake off his mate Joey, for he was

still steamed up, wanting to rip the fuck out of Roy Shaw there and then. He knew that with his thunderous bare fists he stood every chance of felling Roy Shaw who was still wearing the boxing gloves.

Eventually, however, finding his way barred, Lenny calmed down and left the ring to the cheers and jeers of hundreds of fight fans around the ring. He didn't know if they were cheering him on or jeering him. So he put up two fingers to all the fight fans and the whole place roared back, some with approval, some angry at McLean's interruption to their hero's moment of glory.

But Lenny didn't care a fuck for any of the fans. He went home with a smile on his face knowing that his day would come. After watching Shaw smash his opponent in double-quick time, Lenny knew that when it came to his turn, he would have a real fight on his hands. He couldn't wait for that day to dawn.

The title that mattered, the biggest name among London's underworld hard men was, without doubt, 'The Guv'nor'. When news broke that a fight in a ring would be staged between McLean and Shawey, London's fight fans went ballistic trying to obtain tickets. Black-market touts did a roaring trade as the contest approached and unofficial bookmakers were taking bets of thousands of pounds from eager punters willing to back their man with fistfuls of notes.

CHAPTER 2

Lenny McLean was proud that he was born in Hoxton because that little area of London's East End turned out more villains than anywhere in the British Isles. And Lenny meant *real* villains, like the Krays for example, not the soft, mean toe-rags, the plastic gangsters.

He grew up when Hoxton was still a village, a close-knit community where everyone talked to each other, knew each other's business and shared their lives. Everyone was in the same boat – skint and half-starved – but everyone trusted each other. What little unskilled work was available was badly paid. Everyone went hungry at one time or another and people scraped a living, surviving hand-to-mouth. It was a tough old life and everyone realised it.

The only way many people managed to keep their heads above water was by thieving, a bit of villainy or working in the black economy where the tax man never ventured.

Lenny had a wonderful childhood. His mum and dad made him feel loved, warm and happy. The whole family, including his two sisters and two kid brothers, enjoyed their lives together and Lenny's dad brought in enough money for them all to eat and dress well and pay the rent on their new East End council flat in Kent Street, Bethnal Green.

Lenny's dad earned money any way he could; a bit of thieving, flogging knock-off gear and running for the local bookies.

But Lenny's magical, wonderful home life was to be short-lived. He had no idea his father had been given only two years to live after a germ he picked up in India during the war seriously damaged a heart valve. The father who had served in the Royal Marines, whom Lenny called 'Superman', who was always laughing and joking, was suddenly gone. Lenny arrived home one day to find his mother in tears and his father's armchair empty.

Then Jim Irwin, a mountain of a man, entered Lenny's young life, and married his mum. Within weeks of the marriage, brutality and violence became a part of Lenny's life. In his first ferocious attack on the young boy, the arrogant bastard Irwin threw Lenny across the room, breaking his leg and his kneecap. Lenny was just five years old.

Irwin would take a sadistic delight in punishing the children, making them all stand in a line before giving them a belt for any mistakes they had made during the week. But his beltings weren't simply across the arse. He would punch the poor young kids – none of whom were yet teenagers – in the face and all over their bodies. He would also kick them in the stomach.

And when Lenny's mum tried to intervene, the bastard turned on her, punching and kicking her. After one such attack, Lenny's mum suffered five broken ribs and heavy bruising to her face. He simply walked away, leaving her lying half-conscious on the floor.

And when the hated Irwin did use a belt on the kids, he would hit them across the naked arse with the buckle end, perhaps 20 or 30 times, until the skin was a bleeding pulp, and the child a screaming, quivering wreck.

But that appalling, brutal treatment at the hands of a sadist was one of the reasons Lenny eventually became the hardest bastard in London. After his baby brother was belted until nearly unconscious, Lenny, then only eight, waited until Irwin and his mother had gone to sleep and then crept out of the house and took baby Raymond to his nan's two miles away. His nan not only called the police but, more importantly, called Uncle Jimmy, then recognised as one of the toughest men in Hoxton.

Uncle Jimmy was built like an ox, with powerful shoulders and arms and a reputation no one dared argue with. He weighed 21 stone and was 5ft 9in tall, but he was also a real fighter. He was known as a 'ten-man' job because it needed ten men to bring him down. When he saw the gruesome injuries the bastard step-father had given to baby Raymond, Uncle Jimmy saw red and immediately ran round to the flat like a raging bull. He punched down the front door and went straight for Irwin. He punched the living daylights out of Irwin, hitting him with all the force in his mighty body until the bastard lay unconscious on the floor, his face a mass of blood. But Uncle Jimmy wasn't yet ready to quit. He took out his cut-throat razor intending to cut Irwin's face to pieces, but was stopped by Lenny's mother.

When Irwin regained consciousness, Uncle Jimmy ordered him out of the flat. And he promised the cruel bastard that if he ever heard he had returned to the flat, he would smash fuck out of him and then cut his face to pieces. Irwin grabbed his gear and walked out of the flat shaking with fear.

But that series of events, with Uncle Jimmy showing that a real hard bastard can also be a hero, never left Lenny's mind. Lenny looked up to the man who had saved the family from a life of terror; he was proud of him. It was later that Lenny discovered that his uncle Jimmy was known as 'the Guv'nor of Hoxton' and it was years later that Lenny realised that his ambition to become the Guv'nor had begun in those far-off days of childhood.

Lenny determined to follow in his uncle's footsteps, defending the weak and the helpless, particularly children, from cruel, violent bastards like his step-father and dreamed that, one day, he, too, would become the Guv'nor of Hoxton.

But Lenny's mother found life on her own with five children extremely difficult and she pleaded with her brother Jimmy to let the bastard Irwin back in the flat.

He returned and so did the beatings, but they weren't as bad as they had been, though Irwin would sometimes punch and kick the poor, defenceless kids. Lenny learned to live with the violent Irwin, but he couldn't wait to grow up so that he could care for his brothers and sisters and his mum.

As he wrote his famous autobiography *The Guv'nor*, much of what he forced himself to remember from those early days brought a lump to his throat. But it also made him passionate about protecting the weak from the bullies.

Lenny learned to accept the beatings, and the experience hardened him. But there was also a soft side to the lad. Lenny would often talk to a photograph of his dad and, for many years, believed that, one day, he would walk through the door, throw out Irwin, and the whole family would live happily together once again.

It was not to be, and Lenny's day-dreaming was forgotten as he turned his young teenage life to more exciting events, like making the odd quid by thieving and bits and pieces of villainy. By 13, Lenny was 'at it' with a team of young tearaways nicking odds and ends and selling them to neighbours. Within no time, of course, they were nicked and then Lenny and a mate were pulled by two coppers and Lenny was carrying an old bayonet, a bayonet with an edge like a sharp knife. He was given three years in an Approved School.

Two years after getting out of the Approved School, Lenny was grassed up for doing some thieving and he was sent off to Borstal. He was just 17 and had to face another 20 months inside.

When he came out, young Lenny was a very fit, very

well-built young man with powerful shoulders and arms. His life as a hard man was about to start. Whenever any team in Hoxton needed a bit of aggression on a job, Lenny was brought in; if anyone needed a strong man on a job Lenny was brought in; if there was serious violence needed on some cruel bastard, Lenny was the man. His reputation was growing fast and he was earning good money.

The money was mainly – in fact, almost exclusively – derived from villainy, stealing copper, lead and scrap metal and selling it at a handsome profit. He also earned more than a few bob playing the heavy, turning up on request in case trouble flared. Lenny usually earned his money by not hitting or slapping anyone, but just standing there looking aggressive and menacing. But, on occasions, he would find himself out-numbered and he would need all his brute strength and hammer-blow fists to see off the opposition.

Like many an East End villain, Lenny decided that he should earn a regular income rather than relying on the odd job cropping up, so he decided to turn his hand to a little bit of protection. He settled on pubs and quickly became a friend of a number of publicans who, inexplicably, found their pubs coming under attack from mobs of drunken young thugs. They were only too happy to pay him £500 a week to keep the thugs at bay.

For Lenny, it was really easy money because he was the one arranging the punch-ups! As soon as the landlord asked Lenny to mind the place for him, the trouble stopped dead, as if by magic. As a result, other landlords called in Lenny and all discovered that peace and profits returned as soon as Lenny was signed up to mind the place. Lenny called this business his 'pension'.

Sometimes, young tearaways would want to prove themselves in front of their mates and would decide to take on Lenny. As a result, Lenny would sometimes find himself having three scuffles a night. They were all short and sweet.

That too didn't last long because a publican grassed to the police and they gave Lenny an ultimatum: 'Either fuck off from Hoxton to another area or we'll fit you up. Get it?'

Lenny took the advice, moved to Bethnal Green and found it was the best move he had ever made in his young life. As if by accident, Lenny McLean was on his way to becoming the greatest streetwarrior London had ever known.

Within months, Lenny could boast, 'Ask anyone who's seen me fight. Does Lenny ever back off? No. He keeps moving all the time. Does Lenny ever react or flinch when he's taken a punch? No. He feels nothing. He just dishes it out.

'Anyone taking me on was putting a loaded gun to their head, but it never stopped them trying because they all thought, One day he'll be put down and I want to be the one who does it.'

Undeniably, Lenny became an unbelievable fighter. And those who knew him well, those who fought him, believed the reason was not just his remarkable physique, his daunting physical presence, but what was going on inside his head.

And although Lenny never accepted that his brutal step-father Jim Irwin was responsible for anything positive in his life, it is an inescapable fact that much of Lenny's character was formed in those years when he had to confront the despicable, bullying Irwin.

As Lenny put it once, 'After what that beast did to me, and no matter what punch, kick or gouge was directed at me, I never flinched, never backed away.'

Lenny's secret seems to have been that he had somehow found a way during his boyhood years to cope with physical pain, the pain inflicted by Irwin.

He reflected, 'I was pounded and belted by Irwin until I didn't feel a thing.'

But that constant physical pain had made Lenny a very angry young man. When it came to inflicting pain on another fighter, Lenny would say, 'Every punch I ever gave was for that little baby I used to be, who couldn't fight back.'

On the outside, Lenny had become impervious to pain, but on the inside he was a burning cauldron of controlled anger.

There was only one area in which Lenny needed to train – he had to learn to use his fists. So he started shadow boxing, practising in front of a mirror, flashing his fists towards the reflection – one-two, one-two, one-two – until his fists were almost a blur.

And Lenny had also witnessed beyond the legitimate confines of the professional ring. He knew that proper boxing, 'legit' boxing, was licensed and ruled by the British Board of Boxing Control, the fight being managed by a referee who made sure the boxers kept to the strict Queensberry Rules.

But Lenny had been attracted to unlicensed boxing in which both men, wearing regulation boxing gloves, climbed into a ring under the supervision of a referee and battled it out for as many rounds as the opponents agreed beforehand.

At about that time, Lenny met a Cockney fella named Kenny Mac, a second-hand car dealer, who offered to find Lenny a few bare-knuckle fights through which they could both earn some dosh. Kenny agreed to put up the money – £500 – and they would halve any winnings. To Lenny, skint as ever, the deal sounded great.

Lenny was won over to bare-knuckle fighting after he saw his first real fight. He realised he was watching the sport of the hardest men in the *real* world and he wanted to be a part of it. He also realised that, in bare-knuckle fighting, only one man wins, the loser getting nothing whatsoever – no purse, no expenses, not even a few quid for plasters. Both sides put up an agreed amount of money and whoever won took the lot, no questions asked.

And Lenny decided that at 6ft 2in tall, 16 stone, fit as a fiddle and with lightning fists, he must stand a chance. He did.

His first fight lasted ten seconds! Lenny only hit the gypsy once, smashing through his opponent's guard and hitting him with all his might full in the face. For that, Lenny earned £500. He was delighted.

Most of those early fights were against gypsies who thrived on bare-knuckle boxing, not just hoping to make money on the side-bets but the fact that they loved to have a hero, a champion, someone they could say was part of their family. They liked winning good money as well, but they were also in the fight game to enhance the family's reputation and honour.

'Bollocks to all that,' Lenny remarked when asked about fighting for honour, 'I'm in it for the bleedin' money, fuck everything else.'

So Lenny continued to take on all-comers but he was winning every damn fight. His bank balance was doing fine and he hardly had a mark on his face, unlike the poor bastards he was smashing unconscious. Most of his bare-knuckle fights only lasted two or three minutes, and never more than five.

But Lenny was doing too well. As a result, the gypsies and other dare-devils started fighting shy of the Cockney kid who never seemed to lose. So they would only bet £500 a fight at the most and Lenny sometimes found himself fighting for even less.

Once, but only once, some gypsies decided they weren't going to pay Lenny and that was when they had brought in one of the strongest gypsies in Britain to take him on. They laid down a £10,000 wager and Kenny Mac matched it. This was real money and Lenny could see the fella was fit, strong and hard. But the fella made a mistake. As Lenny walked into the area where the bare-knuckle fight was to take place, the gypsy called Lenny a 'fucking wanker'. Though he was still dressed in his everyday clothes, Lenny turned on him in a fury.

The gypsy had been leaning against a window and was taken totally by surprise as Lenny tore into him. After five or six heavy punches, the gypsy went down but Lenny wasn't finished yet. As the gypsy tried to get to his feet, Lenny kicked him full in the face and sent him sprawling. The gypsy tried to protect his face with his hands so Lenny sat on his chest and smashed fuck out of the man's hands until the blood was dripping down his face, his shoulders and his chest. Only then did Lenny get off the man's chest and walk away.

But the gypsy's friends and family refused to pay up because Lenny had jumped the gun. 'Fuck your money,' one said, 'you took him when he weren't ready.'

'Don't tell me to fuck the money,' Lenny shouted in a fury at the man before striking him full in the face, knocking him spark out.

That set the other gypsies alight and five turned on Lenny, who remembers that tear-up well. 'I nutted the first one bang in the mouth and his false teeth flew out. Then I just waded into the remaining four. The last one still standing put his hand up in surrender but I gave him one hard punch in the mouth to teach him a lesson. I look around and they're all over the place, lying down, slumped in corners and one leaning against the shed looking blank.'

Before Lenny and his mate Kenny, his so-called manager and promoter, left the scene, they were promised that the money would be handed over that night.

Right on schedule, the gypsies turned up at Kenny's place at 4.00am, but carrying shooters instead of money. They told Kenny that if Lenny wanted his money, he would have to come and get it. A scared Kenny immediately phoned Lenny, telling him what was going on.

Not caring a damn for his own safety, Lenny quickly dressed, jumped in his car and was at the gypsy camp within 20 minutes. He was owed money and he was determined to get it.

Fortunately, Lenny knew that the geezer with the loot had no wife or kids but lived in a lovely trailer. He arrived at the parking lot, nipped over the fence and walked very quietly to the trailer hoping he hadn't woken any guard dogs. All was quiet.

Lenny took a deep breath, grabbed the door of the trailer, ripped it off its hinges in one heave and, before the fella had time to get out of bed, Lenny had his hand round his neck demanding the money he was owed.

'I want my ten grand now or, on my lad's life, I'm going to smash you to fucking death.'

Lenny wasn't kidding or exaggerating; he was deadly serious. The fella, stark bollock naked, got out of his bunk, his frail legs shaking, went over to a fancy cut-glass cabinet and pulled out a roll of notes. But he only handed over seven big ones, so Lenny threatened him again. Shaking like a leaf, he found another stash of notes behind the stove and handed them over. He was so nervous that he accidentally handed over another six grand, but Lenny gave him back the extra three, telling him, 'I'm just collecting a debt; this ain't no robbery.'

Lenny's life was looking up. He and his darling wife Val now had two children, Jamie and Kelly, and their home was always full of laughter and happiness. Len adored the woman he called 'my Val' and whom he was proud to call his life and his strength. From the moment they met in the Standard pub in Kingsland Road, they had been inseparable although Val was only 17 at the time, a short, pretty girl with blonde hair. They married exactly one year after they'd met and were a wonderfully happy couple.

No matter what trouble Lenny found himself in, Val always stood by him, encouraging and supporting him. She didn't much like the fact he earned his money as a streetwarrior, despite the fact that he was the toughest, hardest man in Britain. She always feared that, as he grew older, he might one day meet someone stronger, fitter, younger and harder and Val knew the sort of damage bare-knuckle fighters did to each other. She hated the thought that her Lenny would one day get really hurt.

She preferred Lenny to do his everyday job, looking after pubs and clubs in the East End. She knew he sometimes had trouble on his hands, but most people disappeared from sight when they heard Lenny McLean was on his way to sort out the problem. Most villains around the East End knew Lenny well and would never try it on, but there were occasional tearaways from outside the manor who believed they were tough and wanted to prove it by tackling Lenny himself. Those wannabes might swing a punch at him and, within seconds, they would wish they hadn't as Lenny's fist crashed into their face sending them reeling and spitting blood, and often their teeth as well. And Lenny earned good money at that game, taking home a good wage packet every week.

But he still had ambition; he still wanted to earn the title he coveted above all else – the Guv'nor.

CHAPTER 3

One of the great streetwarriors of all time was Roy Shaw, a true Cockney, born within the sound of Bow Bells. The ragamuffin, street urchin Roy would wander the streets of the East End searching for dog-ends which he would happily take home to his dad who rolled his own.

Born in 1936, Roy was packed off to the country along with thousands of other London kids when German bombs began to rain down daily on the capital. But he was more fortunate than most kids, the whole family being evacuated to Chippenham in Wiltshire where he spent his childhood in the beautiful countryside running wild with two Labrador dogs for hours at a time.

Before the end of the war, Roy returned to London with his family and was shocked to see half the East End reduced to rubble, whole streets had disappeared and landmarks gone. It seemed like a foreign land.

And at ten, Roy Shaw encountered personal horror and anguish when his beloved father died in a motorbike accident. Now, young Roy was more alone than ever, for since his return to London, life at school had been one long agony. Roy was little for his age and the school bullies picked on him relentlessly.

Each day after school, they would chase him, push him around, belt him, even kick him and leave him on the ground distraught and in tears. After school each day, Roy would run like hell to try and get home before the bullies could catch him. But they were older and faster and, most days, Roy would end up taking a belting from four or six young louts.

The day Roy returned to school after his father's funeral the bullies returned. He ran to escape them but they caught him, encircled him and began to push him around, the customary prelude to a beating. But this time, something happened inside Roy's young head. He felt anger. He felt angry that his dad had died and had been taken away from him, and now he had to look after himself. He also felt anger at the young thugs taunting him, the bully boys who always ran around in a gang, and made life hell for kids like him.

Well, suddenly, he had had enough.

He lashed out at the nearest bully, a lad some years older and hit him smack on the jaw, knocking him backwards. It was the first time Roy had ever struck back at the teenage bullies. In that moment, he had seen that he could retaliate. Another stepped forward and Roy punched him in the face; then a third taunted him and

Roy ran at him, punching him in the mouth. The others began to back off but Roy hadn't finished. He went after them, lashing out at each and every one of them. He was angry, bitterly angry at everything they had done to him over the months and years, terrifying him on a daily basis, making his life a misery, hitting and kicking him until they had had their fun. Now he realised that they were scared of him. One boy against eight. He hit as many as hard as he could until they turned and ran.

On that day, the young Roy had lost his fear of bullies and gained an inner strength. From that day, Roy was never again frightened, never scared and he never ran away from anyone. As a result, he started to do better at school and the bullies kept well clear.

Fortunately for Roy, his dad's brother, Uncle Alf, a boxing fanatic, took him under his wing and they would go down to the local gym in the evening. One day, Uncle Alf suggested that Roy might like to have a tear-up in the local boxing booth and Roy leapt at the idea. To his delight and surprise, he won with a knock-down and earned himself £3 in prize money. Roy was on his way.

He began training seriously and was coached. By the age of 16, Roy had won the Area Championship, the Essex Championship and the Schoolboy Championship trophies which were held at the Albert Hall. Those victories brought Roy great confidence in himself, as well as self-respect. He earned money by going to every nearby boxing booth with his uncle Alf and won nearly every contest.

Like most other teenagers, Roy was called up for National Service at the age of 18 and the discipline of army service was too much for young Roy. He rebelled, got punished and then discovered that the Army was very keen on boxing. So for some months he was the hero, winning fight after fight. But Roy found it almost impossible to accept the authority of NCOs and other senior ranks and would end up in deep shit as he would invariably resort to violence in his anger and frustration. He was admitted to a German lunatic asylum, subjected to eight ECT (electroconvulsive therapy) sessions and was eventually given a dishonourable discharge from the Army for being mad!

Roy didn't care a damn. He knew he wasn't mad but suspected that the Army was!

His progression towards becoming the toughest man in Britain continued apace. After being nicked for robbing a bookie of £3,000, he was sent to Borstal but his fists never stopped working. He knocked out the two hardest men who were running the place and took control of the whole set-up. The Borstal was a haven of peace and quiet because Roy refused to allow any bullying. And the Governor respected him for it.

But Roy was fed up with life at Borstal and made his escape. For three months he remained on the run, but in that time he met Mickey Duff – who knew nothing of his escape – who signed him up after watching Roy stop two competent boxers in their tracks.

Roy began training at the famous Thomas a' Beckett in the Old Kent Road under the renowned trainer Danny Holland. Roy found himself training with Terry Spinks (who went on to win an Olympic gold medal) and Terry Downs, who later brought the World Middleweight title back to Britain.

By day, Roy worked in a chair factory and trained at

the Thomas a' Beckett at night. He was learning fast. And, as he was still on the run from Borstal, he changed his name to Roy West.

Under Mickey Duff's management, Roy had ten fights in ten weeks, six ending in KOs. The newspaper headlines, read DREAM DEBUT OF NEW FIGHTER. Later, Mickey Duff would say, 'Roy Shaw was one of the most promising prospects I had ever had at that time in my career.'

But the law caught up with Roy and he ended up doing three years in Maidstone Jail with such notorious criminals as Frankie Fraser, Jimmy Andrews and Jimmy Essex.

In 1959, Roy walked to freedom once more and instantly fell in love with Carolina, a darling, sweet, innocent 17-year-old Maltese girl whose parents ran a restaurant in Aldgate. He wanted to carry her away, spoil her, care for her and marry her. But that required money and Roy was stoney broke. He didn't fancy working for £10 a week at a regular job so villainy seemed the only way of earning good money quickly.

Roy was invited to join a seven-man firm of specialists who earned their living carrying out good little blags knocking off cars taking the wages from the banks to their factories. Each man had a specific task in this team.

Later, Roy explained his role: 'I was employed to stop the car and dish out any violence if it became necessary. I used to stand on a corner wearing a rolled-up balaclava and holding a house brick wrapped up in newspaper under my arm. I hid an Indian club up my left sleeve. I looked like an ordinary working man waiting on the side of the road to be picked up by a mate.

'As soon as the car came into view, I rolled down the

balaclava, ran into the middle of the road and hurled the brick through the car's windscreen. From a side-road, our ramming car would race out, smashing at speed into the side of the wages car, stopping it in its tracks. I would run up to the car, swinging my Indian club and yelling at the passengers not to move a muscle. Within seconds, another member of the team would have the boot open and we would be running away to our getaway cars.'

The firm were so successful that they travelled together all over the country hitting wages vehicles. By moving to different locations all the time, the local police were powerless to catch them because they had no information. Within a few weeks, Roy had a nice new motor, a nice few quid in his pocket and the attention of the beautiful Maltese girl he adored. He was riding high.

By accident and a moment's madness, Roy became involved in a robbery at a bakery in Stepney in 1961 and ended up being banged up for 21 months. There he met Jack 'The Hat' McVitie, a notorious criminal and fearless brawler, and Frank 'Mad Axeman' Mitchell, who was sentenced to life in Dartmoor because Broadmoor refused to have him, believing him to be far too dangerous. He was sprung by the Kray twins, Ronnie and Reggie, and taken to a safe house, a flat in Barking. Frustrated at being 'imprisoned' in a tiny flat, Frank made demands on the Kray twins. One night, the twins agreed to move him. He stepped into the back of a van on Christmas Eve 1966 and was never seen again. Roy knows the truth – Frank was shot dead. He also knows who did it, although Frank Mitchell's body has never been found.

But Roy Shaw's run of bad luck would continue with a vengeance. With nine other fellas he carried out a daring armed raid on a security van in Longfield, Kent, in 1963, in which £87,000 was stolen, equivalent to about £2,000,000 today. But Roy and the others were grassed up and he was given 18 years inside.

In Wandsworth, Roy palled up with Ronnie Biggs who had just been given 30 years for his part in the Great Train Robbery. Biggsy offered to spring him for £10,000, but while Roy was thinking whether to accept the offer, he was moved to Parkhurst on the Isle of Wight. He hadn't been there more than a few months when news came through that Biggsy had gone over the wall. The news was met with great cheers from all the Parkhurst cons.

But life for Roy was tough. He felt that his marriage was falling apart and that his beloved Carolina would give him the elbow, unable to take 18 years with her husband in the slammer. As he said later, 'It's assumed that it's glamorous being married to a gangster – all fur coats and no knickers – but the reality is spending all day travelling to a prison in the middle of nowhere and standing outside in the rain waiting to have the humiliation of being searched, only to have a moany old bastard barking at you for two hours. There's more to life for a young woman than that.'

Roy really loved his Carolina and his two kids and inside Parkhurst he missed all of them deeply. He would say later, 'I felt terrible for Carolina. I missed her so much when I was banged up. I've always found the soppy stuff hard to express, but Carolina seemed to understand that, and for the first time I felt someone loved me just as I was. Nothing seemed to put her off; she took it all in her stride, and her love meant the world to me.'

But after two years in Parkhurst, Roy Shaw knew that

the marriage was at an end. During her visits, Carolina was looking more lovely with fresh make-up, well-groomed hair – obviously someone enjoying life. Roy knew she must have a man in her life. After that visit, Roy cracked, lost control and went berserk when ten screws tried in vain to restrain him. Many went down as Roy tore into them, swinging the iron cosh he had made from smashing apart a water pipe. The end came when one managed to inject him and he was sent off to the cuckoo's nest, the funny farm, the loony bin; in other words, Broadmoor.

After five years in Broadmoor, Roy won the right to be moved back to Parkhurst. It was 1970 and Roy had been banged up for seven years. Then he was moved to Gartree Prison near Leicester and then to Durham Jail. But it didn't stop there. Roy was moved from jail to jail like a fucking shuttlecock.

Finally, Roy was free once more and he had no intention of ever returning to jail again. It was 1973 and Roy was still a young, fit man of 37. But he needed to get some money together fast so that he could start to enjoy life to the full. There was only one problem; all Roy's training throughout his life had been connected with violence. And the East End respected Roy for excelling in four particular areas – boxing, street-fighting, bare-knuckle fighting and protecting people's property.

He hadn't been back on his old manor ten minutes when he got a call from an old mate running a club in Dagenham. Some tough fellas called the Maxwell brothers were causing trouble, demanding money, frightening customers and scaring the staff. One day, Roy walked into the club and introduced himself to the Maxwell boys in a pleasant, chatty way.

'Hi,' he said, 'I'm Roy Shaw; can I buy you a drink?'

They looked at him, checking him out. Roy went on, 'There are going to be some changes round here. From now on, I'm running this place. If you want to argue with that, now's your chance.'

They nodded, finished their drinks and walked out, never to return. The owner happily gave Roy a large bonus but, more importantly, word quickly spread throughout Essex and East London that Roy Shaw had returned to the scene and cleaned up clubs without anyone getting hurt. Offers from clubs far and wide came streaming in, asking Roy simply to stop by and put his name to their club. His name became a magical byword for peace and prosperity among club owners.

Every night became party night for Roy. He would visit 'his' clubs, eating in one, having a drink in another, chatting to mates in a third and partying in all of them. He was also greeted with enthusiasm by the club owners and the regulars and, more importantly, every week he would collect wicked amounts of money from all of them.

As Roy put it, 'Violence had always been a part of my life, but now, I was getting paid for preventing violence and I loved it.'

But Roy was a born fighter and he still looked forward to a good scrap, particularly if he got paid handsomely for it as well. It wasn't long before the lure of bare-knuckle fighting, Roy's favourite money-spinner, became too much.

An old friend called Ronnie Smith heard that Roy was on the scene once again and phoned to tell him about

Barnet Fair, the once-a-year gypsy shindig which included horse-trading, cock-fighting and the gypsy's favourite sport, bare-knuckle bouts. Roy was even more interested when he heard the prize money amounted to £2,000.

Roy and Ron made their way to the circle of men gathered between the large, expensive, chromed trailers. There were ten to twelve hard-looking young men – the warriors – waiting for their moment of glory, victory in a bare-knuckle fight which would bring them honour, prestige and money.

The young fighters, and the scores of men gathered round for the spectacle, eyed Roy closely as he walked into the middle of the area.

'I'll challenge anyone of you,' he said. 'I'll take on the best.'

His brash challenge was met with cat-calls and yelps of delight for the on-lookers believed this outsider, whom none of them had seen before, was about to get his arse kicked by one of their own.

Roy and the gypsy who had been selected to take him on both took off their jackets and shirts and, stripped to the waist, took up positions opposite each other. There was, of course, no ring, no preliminaries, no boxing gloves and no referee. Just a cheering, baying mob of scores of men who had wagered hundreds of pounds on the outcome of the fight.

The young gypsy sprang towards Roy, expecting to knock the stuffing out of him in a welter of flailing fists and arms. Roy stayed calm and picked off the strong-looking lad who had obviously fancied his chances against a man who looked around 40 years of age. Five times the young man attacked him, and five times Roy side-stepped and then gave him fierce, crashing punches to his stomach and his head. In two minutes, the fight was over and Roy had made himself a grand.

'Anyone else?' Roy called out as the young lad's mates took their beaten hero away to recover.

Another gypsy strippped to the waist and, before the fight began, the bets were changing hands all round the circle of men. Roy saw hundreds of pounds being wagered. Another young gypsy, named Elijah Boy, looked stronger and more of a fighter and this fight was not as easy for Roy.

Elijah Boy could box and he knew how to side-step, feint and counter-punch. He didn't just come roaring in like a mad bull and Roy had to take some hard knocks before finally unleashing a torrent of punches which all but knocked the Boy unconscious. Roy had won again and earned himself another £1,000.

Roy didn't move and everyone waited in expectation as Elijah Boy was taken away. Roy took some deep breaths, regaining his strength and his composure and then issued a third challenge to anyone prepared to take him on. He was feeling strong and confident.

One more young gypsy stripped off to a round of cheers and yells from his many mates but he wasn't good enough to tangle with Roy. Within two minutes, the lad had been knocked backwards five times and it would have been silly for him to continue. Roy had won another £1,000.

Ron drove a very happy Roy Shaw back home. He had £3,000 in his pocket and hardly a mark on his face or body. He was well satisfied with his day's work.

NICHOLAS DAVIES / 40

Roy had now been accepted in Essex and East London as The Guv'nor, the undisputed champion of bare-knuckle boxing, who was also respected as the best man around to keep trouble out of clubs and pubs. Mere mention of his name now struck terror into the hearts of young tearaways who thought they could take him on and win. Occasionally, one or two young wannabes tangled with Roy who swatted them as though they were flies. If they threw a couple of punches at Roy, he would retaliate immediately, knocking seven shades out of them for daring to challenge him. He was determined to retain the title of The Guv'nor and had no intention of letting some youngster think there was any way that anyone could challenge and defeat Roy Shaw.

Before the championship of all championships took place – the fight with Lenny McLean – there was one other serious challenge that Roy had to face against a man whom Roy didn't like one bit.

Donny 'The Bull' Adams was a man like Roy himself; hard, strong, fit and quick. Adams had a wicked record – 48 fights and 48 victories! He would tour gypsy fairs, throw down challenges and walk away with wads of money. He was well-known as the King of the Gypsies. He revelled in the title. But Roy saw Adams as an animal that needed taming and he would be the one to tame him.

The contest between Roy and Adams was no quick challenge at a gypsy fair. It was a battle which caught the imagination of all those who loved their boxing to be ferocious and violent, billed as a fight to the death on all the posters. This was the one bare-knuckle fight that had caught the imagination and the pubs and clubs frequented by streetwarriors could talk about nothing else for weeks before the big fight.

The gangster Joey Pyle organised the fight, printed the tickets and put up the posters. The venue was a major headache because no hall could be hired for an unlicensed, bare-knuckle boxing match. The reason – in Britain it is illegal for any boxer to fight without gloves. In the end, they agreed to fight in the open air at a farm in Herefordshire.

The first 1,000 £5 tickets sold within days and another 1,000 were printed and sold within days as well. Already that meant there was £10,000 in the pot in the winner-takes-all competition. In fact, tickets for the fight were changing hands for £10 a time as the day drew closer.

But the Old Bill stepped in and Donny and Roy were taken to court in Hereford in October 1975 and bound over to keep the peace for one year. To get around the problem, they agreed to hold the fight under Queensberry Rules and to wear lightweight gloves. The fight could go ahead.

The newspapers had now been alerted to the fight and they saw the contest as turning the sporting clock back 100 years. Interest in the fight sent the black market price for the tickets to £25. And side-bets were being wagered in monkeys and grands.

As the day of the fight approached, the more frenzied was the public interest, some newspapers slagging off Joey Pyle for staging a fight 'to the death'; others demanded that the police step in to stop the fight; some newspapers even called on the Government to halt such a dangerous sport. Adams and Roy even appeared on *The Eamonn Andrews Show* and he asked both of them, 'If the fight does take place, will you really fight to the death?'

There was a long pause and then, totally unrehearsed, they both replied 'Yes' at the same time. There were gasps from the audience and then everyone fell silent. You could hear a pin drop.

Now there was no need to fight in secret in the open air – offers of venues came from many organisations including a number of top football clubs. But the best offer, which they jumped at, came from Billy Smart who offered them a big top circus tent at Winkfield, Berkshire. Now there was no stopping the contest and Joey printed hundreds more tickets, the best selling for £20 each. They were well and truly in the money.

It was just before this fight that the *Sun* gave Roy his nickname 'Pretty Boy' because they said he was such a handsome devil. As Roy commented, 'I didn't know if the *Sun* was taking the piss or not; I had been called many things in my time but "pretty" – never.'

The night of the fight – 1 December 1975 – was a dark, stormy night with the wind howling a gale and the rain lashing down. As Adams and Roy stepped into the ring to thunderous applause, a large, brawny Irishman broke through the security cordon and clambered on to the ropes, bellowing that he wanted to fight both of them. Adams and Roy grabbed him and threw him out again where he was grabbed by security guards and carried away bawling his head off.

'Nosher' Powell, a former boxer, bouncer, minder and stunt man, was the Master of Ceremonies and introduced the fighters:

'Ladies and gentlemen, the bout everybody has been

waiting for. In the red corner, introducing Donny "The Bull" Adams, tipping the scales at 14st 6lb, fighting out of Waltham Cross, North London.

'And in the blue corner, introducing Roy "Pretty Boy" Shaw, weighing in at 15st 11lb from Dagenham, Essex.'

The referee called the fighters together as the crescendo of noise reverberated around the big top. 'I want you to touch gloves then please yourselves.'

Later, Roy would recall exactly what happened from the moment the bell went:

'I was exploding with energy. Adams rushed at me and I hit him once on the chin with a right while he was standing up; twice more on the chin while he was on one knee, and twice more while he was on the floor. I kicked him in the ribs as hard as I could and then lifted him up so I could knock him down again. I was so pumped up with adrenalin and energy I really wanted to kill him. There was no count from the referee, just an extraordinary uproar from the fight fans, as I continued to smash, pummel and kick his prone body.

'The crowd hissed, spat and jeered as I jumped on Adams' head. Adams didn't move. He was out cold.

'I would have continued to smash the bastard but the referee, aided by the marshals who had jumped into the ring, hauled me off him before I could kill him. The referee raised my hand in the air declaring me the winner and the fans went wild.

'Adams was still lying on the floor, half-unconscious. I felt nothing for him, nothing. He was dead meat as far as I was concerned.

'But the fans were angry that their hero had put up such a pathetic fight. They began shouting and jeering, yelling at him to get up and fight on. But there was no fight left in him. Fed up and angry, his supporters turned on those yelling for me and fights and scuffles broke out, bottles were thrown, punches were thrown and I could see from my vantage point in the ring that there could be serious trouble brewing. I knew a lot of the crowd were well pissed and Adams' supporters were really pissed off.

'Fortunately, someone had the sense to switch on the main lights and the crowd finally realised the fight was over and there was no point in continuing the scuffles. The violence stopped.'

As Roy sat in his dressing-room towelling down, a dejected, embarrassed-looking Adams walked in. He walked up to Roy and shook him by the hand.

'It was a fair result,' Adams said. 'That means that Roy is now The Guv'nor and that makes him King of London.'

Roy commented afterwards, 'I admired Donny "The Bull" for what he did and what he said to me after the fight. It took a man, a real man, to shake my hand after I had just beaten him so savagely.'

Roy Shaw went home that night a very happy and a very rich man. Though Roy has never revealed how much money he made from that single fight, rumours have suggested that he pocketed around £20,000! In 1975, that was a hell'uva lot of money.

CHAPTER 4

It was the fight of the twentieth century but it didn't take place in a massive arena, like Madison Square Gardens in New York or Wembley Stadium, London, but in a small nightclub in Croydon, South London, before a tiny crowd of 1,000 people. And the men who paid good money to attend that famous fight were all dedicated hard men whose love for bare-knuckle boxing and admiration for those who fought such vicious battles knew no bounds.

This was no hyped world title fight screened live across the world's television networks with tens of millions glued to their TV sets around the globe. Nor would the winner walk away with a multi-million-pound purse. This was a fight to the death by two of the strongest, toughest, most lethal men in Britain – Lenny

McLean and Roy Shaw.

The prize was £3,000 in cash with the winner taking everything and the loser not a penny. More importantly, however, was the fact that the winner also took the most coveted title in London, the right to be called The Guv'nor.

That simple prize meant so much because it was all about intense pride and burning, feverish passion – not just for the two fighters involved, but for everyone who knew the secret underworld of London's hard bastards where no rules apply, no conditions are laid down and no quarter is given. And yet, amongst those dedicated hard bastards everyone knows his place. And the top man is known as The Guv'nor.

These men all respected the three famous 'R's – respect, reputation and a row. Respect is an attitude of deference, admiration, regard, the state of being honoured. Reputation is a generally high opinion held about someone. Row is a hard bastard who fights with determination. It is also a battle, a struggle, physical combat and a punch-up.

Respect for the three 'R's was the single criterion which bound together everyone who attended that famous battle at Sinatra's Night Club in South London.

Those hard bastards are a people apart from the rest of British society. They live by a totally different code of ethics. They all exude aggression. They eat it, sleep it and breathe it. Violence is their life. They are men who live by their wits but which sometimes includes murder, armed robbery, wage-snatches and tons of violence.

But the men who earn the greatest respect among

this strange, tough breed of battle-hardened warriors are those who fight with their hands, the bare-knuckle boxers, the bruisers and battlers who will stand toe-to-toe with another hard bastard determined to knock seven shades of shit out of his opponent. And yet, deep down, both those hard bastards probably have great respect for each other.

There are other hard bastards, however, who dislike each other with a ferocious and undying passion. Some are plain jealous, others have secret fears, still more have a loathing for another hard bastard because of some trivial act or remark which may have been used against him.

Most hard bastards live within the criminal underworld, but not all of them. There are many law-abiding, straight-up tough guys, some of whom are members of the SAS or the Parachute Regiment, boxers, wrestlers, judo and karate experts, bouncers, minders, stunt men, gypsies and, even, some police officers. However, there are not too many coppers in that select group of men, because coppers usually operate mob-handed, which is not the way most hard bastards behave.

The first time that Roy Shaw heard Lenny McLean's name was when a pal phoned him to say he had a fella causing problems in his Hoxton pub in East London. Always happy to help out a mate, Roy Shaw agreed to visit the pub and have a word with 'this McLean fella'. Roy went down and had a pint but there was no sign of Lenny McLean.

Word on the street soon spread that Roy Shaw, renowned as the toughest man in London, was looking for McLean, and that message sent shockwaves through the enthusiasts of bare-knuckle fighting, hoping they would be around when Shaw met McLean. Most people thought such a fracas would probably take place in a pub car park or, maybe, behind some gymnasium or clubhouse. And everyone wanted to be there to witness the two men knocking hell out of each other.

Shaw made enquiries about McLean and most people thought Shaw was mad to want to teach McLean a lesson. Every mention of McLean's name seemed to create tension and not a little fear amongst those Shaw spoke to.

They all said the same: 'He's awesome, he's massive, he's this, he's that ...' But none of those remarks worried Roy Shaw. He had heard worse. A man's size had never worried Roy Shaw. He believed in the old boxing maxim 'the bigger they come, the harder they fall'.

Roy Shaw never did catch up with Lenny McLean until a promoter approached him with a substantial offer and asked whether he would be prepared to have a fight – a bare-knuckle boxing match – with Lenny McLean. Shaw was happy to take on Lenny on one condition. It would be on the strict understanding that the winner took the entire purse, the way fights had been arranged in the bygone years of bare-knuckle boxing.

But Lenny McLean had heard about Roy 'Pretty Boy' Shaw. He had heard a great deal about the man who claimed to be The Guv'nor, the toughest man in London.

Lenny had also seen a large poster of Shaw in a pub

that advertised the match between Shaw and Donny Adams. When Lenny saw that picture of the two contestants, he said, 'See them two. I could do them both in the same night.'

The landlord warned him, 'Take a friendly warning, son ... that Roy Shaw is a lunatic.'

Lenny replied, 'Shut up, you c—t. You're looking at a worse lunatic.'

But the landlord hadn't finished. He replied, 'Yeah, I know all about you, but I know all about Roy Shaw as well.'

The landlord sensed that Lenny really did fancy himself in a fight against Roy Shaw, so he proposed a deal. 'If you want, I'll put the word to Roy. See if he's interested.'

'You do that,' snapped back Lenny, 'I've got the money and he can have the fight on the cobbles or in the ring, with gloves or bare knuckles; either way I'll do him.'

But nothing happened for months and both men were left wondering what the hell was going on. Fellas in the pubs and clubs were talking about the possibility of a match between the two tough men but it was all talk and no action.

One night, Lenny McLean was minding a club when in walked Roy Shaw accompanied by the famous fixer, Joe Pyle. Lenny said later, 'I took note that Roy Shaw seemed a tough-looking geezer with close-set eyes which made him appear mean. Roy seemed like a volcano about to explode. He didn't look as though he was with us, but just stared into his own world with those fucking mean eyes.'

The two men didn't exchange a word.

Joe Pyle then turned to Lenny, saying, 'You know who this is, Lenny, don't you?'

'Yeah,' replied Lenny, 'I know him.'

Lenny agreed to put up £3,000 in prize money, winner takes all, and Roy nodded. Before he left, Roy Shaw said menacingly to Lenny, 'Make sure you're there.'

Lenny McLean decided to find out more about his opponent Roy. He talked to people from Hoxton who had known Roy his entire life and they told Lenny of Roy's background, his family, his hard times, his fights and his reputation as the hardest bastard in London.

As a result, Lenny had a hell'uva lot of respect for Roy Shaw. In his autobiography, *The Guv'nor*, Lenny McLean wrote,

From what I was told about his background, Roy Shaw deserves a good gee (compliment). Like me, his dad died when he was young. He didn't suffer the violence I did, but his early years were the same as mine; bit of thieving, dishing out violence, approved school, Borstal, prison. Before he got tripped up by the law, he'd taken up the gloves, something I have never fancied, and he boxed his way through ten professional fights – ten wins, six KOs. I knew, however, that once you've got a criminal record, that's your licence down the pan. So Roy had to give up any plans for a career in the licensed ring.

So he thinks, Fuck 'em, and starts taking his wages out of banks and security vans with the

help of a shooter. His biggest and last robbery was a nice little earner of £90,000 from a van in Kent. Then he was grassed up and got a 15.

Did he settle down and serve his time? Did he bollocks! He fought every step of the way. If he wasn't fighting other cons it was the screws. Once, when he got a bit upset, he ripped a piece of metal off his bed and smashed his way through the locked cell door. I never heard of anyone else doing that.

Nothing they could do to him slowed him down because he was so full of hate for the system, and I can understand that. The screws did his head in so many times with their truncheons he had more scars than hair, and he still wouldn't let up. So they ghosted him off to Broadmoor. Not because he was a lunatic, but because there was no way they could control him.

Well, Roy worked out that they could bang him up for ever in Broadmoor Hospital, so he kept his head down, behaved himself, and was returned to the prison system and finished his time. That's when he took up unlicensed fighting. In his case, legal robbery.

After I learned everything about his life, I had to give him a lot of respect. He'd suffered, he'd fought against the same fucking system I hate and he's come out the other side. He had to be good stuff. Repecting the way he's handled his life didn't mean that I'd changed my mind about tearing his head off. If he was putting himself on offer, Lenny McLean was going to take it up.

Undeniably, Lenny McLean hardly bothered to get himself in shape for that first title fight with Roy Shaw. Lenny had never trained before in his entire life and he wasn't about to start. He boasted that he never put on an ounce in weight, although every day he put away a dustbin-lid-sized plate of steak, eggs, mushrooms and tomatoes and topped it off with half-a-dozen cream cakes. As a sweetener to his mates, who were backing him to win, Lenny did agree to quit smoking – for a few days!

Lenny had hoped this first fight would be bare knuckle, but there had been so much talk and hype about the match, Joe Pyle, the promoter, ordered both men to wear gloves because of the risk of a police raid. Both Lenny and Roy thought gloves were only for fairies but, somewhat reluctantly, they agreed to wear the crêpe bandages and the old, thin, tired-looking six-ounce gloves they were given to wear. Those lightweight gloves gave such little protection to the two boxers that they might just as well have been fighting without anything. Every time a punch landed, it would be as though no gloves were being used. In other words, those who had ever been involved in bare-knuckle fighting knew just how much pain could be inflicted when struck by either men with the full force of their heavyweight bodies behind the punch.

Nosher Powell, the ultimate hard man, who refereed that first McLean–Shaw fight, commented, 'I knew both men. Lenny McLean was probably the most frightening man I ever knew, but we were mates. Lenny was over

6ft tall and weighed in excess of 20 stone with a 40in waist and a 60in chest. He was huge. He was also very dangerous when he got angry and tended to walk through doors rather than open them.'

He went on, 'I also knew Roy Shaw. He was reputed to be the only man the Kray brothers were genuinely frightened of, and I can well believe it. He was built like a brick shithouse, balding and menacing, with close-set eyes that made him look even meaner.'

Nosher added, 'These two fearsome figures were folklore in South London and seeing them go head-to-head was something no one wanted to miss. Everyone knew it would be a fight with blood and teeth on the canvas.'

Days before the fight, newspapers were carrying stories of the big fight, including quotes from Lenny that he would 'rip Shaw's head off his shoulders'.

The club was packed to the rafters with fans and the atmosphere was charged, the music booming out Gary Glitter's famous song, 'I'm The Leader Of The Gang'.

Lenny waited in his corner for the arrival of Roy Shaw and he came through the crowded hall shoving people out of the way and knocking chairs over. The noise grew to a crescendo, the fans were loving the hype and Roy's aggression. Roy was showing Lenny and all the fans the sort of man he was. He chucked himself all over the place, swinging his arms above his head in salute. He vaulted the three ropes into the ring and stood opposite Lenny jumping and bouncing up and down. Lenny stayed in his corner leaning nonchalantly against the ropes.

In the ring, Lenny looked about twice the size of

'Pretty Boy' Shaw.

Lenny described the pre-fight showmanship. 'Down comes Roy Shaw, shoving people out of the way and knocking chairs over. He might not have been a nutter, but he was some showman who knew how to sell himself. He was chucking himself all over the place and swinging his arms about. I thought to myself that he should be saving his energy for the fight, because I knew he would need it.'

Roy Shaw took one look at Lenny in the ring, stripped to his shorts, and told his corner man, 'Look at the fucking size of him.'

Of course, the two men saw that fight totally differently. Later, they would talk through the fight as they saw it unfold.

Lenny recalled, 'The bell's gone. I steamed straight in and belted him, but the gloves aren't doing me any favours. I wanted to rip the bastard things off because they were breaking my fingers. My fucking gloves kept springing open. Round one – a waste of time.

'Round two wasn't much better, but as I couldn't get a decent punch in to slow him down he'd wedged me in the corner and for the full three minutes he smashed me on the head and the chin.

'Round three was exactly the same. To give him his due, he could throw a wicked punch, but I could take every one of those punches. Bang, bang, bang. He's giving it everything he's got; he's desperate to put me down. He'd be the first one who ever did.

'Come the fourth round and we're both absolutely knackered – me from taking his punches and not being able to retaliate and him because of his non-stop throwing of all his punches. Half-way through the fourth round and I was still laughing at him and calling him names, and that was making him wilder and more exhausted.

'Ding, the bell goes; and the ref's calling it a day. I don't want to make excuses and I don't want to take anything away from Roy. He gave me some punishment that would've flattened anybody else. But he couldn't hurt me and he couldn't put me down. I've got to hold my hand up. I wasn't fit – I was used to the damage I could inflict with bare knuckles inside the first minute of a fight. The gloves didn't help but I let myself down by not being properly prepared.'

Roy saw the fight differently. He said, 'As soon as the first bell sounded, I decided to steam heavily into McLean's belly because he was so tall I knew it would double him up. I hit him with some lovely body shots.

'Then McLean spouted off to the crowds, "Look, he can't hurt me." I stuck one on his chin which soon shut him up, then carried on punching him in the belly to weaken him. By the end of the first round, he was puffing when he staggered back to his corner. I was excited at the wild joy of my own vitality.

'In round two, I constantly attacked and shoved McLean on to the ropes and I knew that I was shaping the fight and giving it momentum. I switched blows from his belly to his chin. McLean never laid a glove on me but I was wearing myself out punching him. At the end of the second round, I was the one puffing.

'I took a large gulp of cold water from the plastic bottle, rinsed my mouth out and spat into the metal bucket.

'The bell went for round three. I only knew one way to fight – going forward. I tracked McLean round the ring like a fox on a hunt but there was nowhere for him to run and nowhere to hide. I was all over him like a rash. I banged him with a right but he had a rock solid chin. McLean was fighting now with desperation, ignoring the blood – his blood. I swung a wide left and a right that wobbled him. He hung on to the ropes and through gritted teeth, hissed, "I've had enough."

'McLean was demoralised, weary and bleeding after my savage attack. He looked to the referee to intervene and I could taste victory. With one final clubbing right hand to the head, the referee stepped in and raised my arm in victory.'

The noise and the mayhem that followed that fight didn't stop with people screaming and yelling for the boxers. Within seconds of Shaw's arm being raised in victory, fights broke out around the ring. McLean's supporters were furious that the fight had been stopped and Shaw's people were wonderfully happy that their man had beaten the great Lenny McLean. Anyone who wanted a fight could have one and they were keen to show they had the same power and aggression as their hero Shaw. The bare-knuckle fights went on for 15 minutes and scuffles were continuing in the street as people finally drifted out of the club to make their way to the nearest pub.

Three of Roy Shaw's supporters, however, went too far – and paid the price. As a dejected Lenny was walking back to his car after the fight, three hefty-looking blokes stood in front of Lenny, barring his way, and began taking the piss. They suggested he was a 'fairy' and his excuse for losing was the problem with his thin gloves. They cracked jokes at Lenny's expense and all began laughing at him. They were also well pissed. Lenny saw red, butted one to the ground and smashed the other two with haymakers. Lenny left all three lying on the ground half-conscious and walked off to his car.

That little fracas made Lenny feel much better. He was back in the real world, his world, where bare knuckles ruled the streets.

Shaw wanted to let the world know that he had not only beaten McLean but he had also kept all the purse. He added, 'I would like to place on the record the fact that McLean earned nothing for that fight with me. Usually, of course, the purse is divided. But the only condition I laid down when agreeing to a fight with McLean was that the winner took the entire purse. And the purse was good.'

But McLean's defeat at the hands of his tormentor Roy Shaw played on his mind and his nerves. McLean was convinced that he could beat Roy Shaw, but very few people shared his confidence. There was no doubt that Shaw had comprehensively beaten McLean, a boxer had taken on a fighter and the boxer had won handsomely.

But McLean was not to be denied a re-match, despite the fact that since facing 'Pretty Boy' Shaw, McLean had fought and lost two further fights against top-flight boxers.

Friends told McLean that if he really was determined to beat Roy Shaw in the ring, he would have to train seriously and get fit, really fit. This time round, Lenny knew that he must take this fight as the most serious of his life if he ever wanted the title he yearned for – the right to call himself the Guv'nor.

Lenny realised how unfit he was after only one hour's training, running round a track. Lenny and a mate named Frank decided to get fit together and after less than half-a-mile the two of them could hardly breathe, let alone run. They decanted to the nearest pub hardly able to speak they were so shattered. But that first training session worked wonders for Lenny. He knew that if he was going to stand a chance of beating Roy – a proper boxer – he would have to get himself in peak condition.

So Lenny began running and, little by little, he found he could run a mile, then two miles and so it went on. But his friends were still worried that Lenny would never stand a cat in hell's chance of beating Roy Shaw in the boxing ring. They knew that if the two men met in a pub car park – bare-knuckle fighting with no holds barred – Lenny would win hand's down. But this second fight would be under the same Queensberry Rules as the first one, and the odds favoured Roy ten to one.

Finally, Lenny agreed to see a trainer, a boxing trainer, to teach him the tricks of the trade – how to defend himself and where and when to attack and counter-punch. For the next eight weeks, Lenny went to the gym every day and a trainer by the name of Freddie put Lenny through his paces, teaching him how to box, not just fight.

Roy Shaw, on the other hand, didn't bother to train or do the hard work running and skipping, toning his body for the big fight. Roy was now over 40 years of age and certainly past his peak. His fights over the years had earned him a good income and he had a substantial amount of capital in the bank. He didn't really need a re-match with Lenny; he didn't really want one.

But Roy Shaw knew the fight game and he understood the lore of bare-knuckle boxing. If someone lost a fight, he was entitled to ask for a re-match. It was also an unwritten rule that the victor of the first fight had to grant the loser one re-match.

Roy Shaw later told of his preparations for the return match. 'I made no preparations for the fight, I didn't change my diet or do any extra training. I had become lazy, a fat-cat. I'd earned more money than I could spend and was just going through the motions.

'Looking back on it now, I must have been mad; I was in my early forties and, like most boxers, I should have given it up while I was on top, but I've got to admit that I didn't know when to quit. Up until that point, I had an unbeaten record and should have realised that I was fighting a man 12 years younger, six inches taller and four stone heavier!

'I had nothing to prove by fighting McLean a second time. I had beaten him once, but agreed to fight him again, just for the hell of it.'

Roy Shaw had been taking ginseng, the root of a medicinal plant from the Far East which is reputed to increase stamina and energy. On his way to the fight, he stopped at a Chinese herbalist and bought a bottle of the stuff. Never before had Roy taken ginseng in liquid form and was totally unaware of its potency. He drank half the bottle.

Later, Roy explained what happened. 'When I arrived at the venue, I felt sluggish and lethargic. I felt as though I had been smoking cannabis. It was a strange feeling. I was aware of everything going on around me – the loud music, the roaring crowds and my corner giving me instructions – but everything seemed in slow motion.

'I climbed into that ring in a daze, as weak as a kitten. The ginseng had taken away all my strength, and now I knew how Samson felt when Delilah cut off his hair. I was so chilled out when the bell rang and McLean came at me like a charging bull, he knocked me down within minutes. It was as easy as taking candy from a baby. I couldn't understand why I was so slow. I'd lost the fight and there was nothing I could do about it. And like other fighters before me, I had to know how to lose with grace and dignity.

'McLean hadn't hurt me physically but he had dented my pride and taken away my precious title. I had learned a lesson that night; nobody, including me, is indestructible.'

Lenny, however, saw the fight differently.

He recalled, 'I sat in the dressing room keyed up and ready to go. On the outside I'm dead calm but inside I'm boiling to get my hands on Roy Shaw. At that moment, I hated him. I wanted to hurt him.

'We came out in the first round and I smashed him down, punched him to the floor. He got up and I immediately smashed him down again. I stamped on him and kicked him. I put the boot in and his corner jumped in the ring, got me round the neck and physically dragged me off him. I could see Shaw was dazed but not done.

'He got to his feet and bang, they let go of me. I steam in. One, two, three, four punches to the head and he went head first through the ropes. Everybody's going arse over bollocks as he sprawls over the first and second row of spectators. I've done him. Up went my hand as the winner.'

But to Lenny McLean, that meant they needed to meet one more time – for the decider. Now they had won one each and Lenny was as keen as mustard to clinch it, to show the world that he was now The Guv'nor.

Lenny had won £25,000 but what he wanted was the decider. As he put it, 'I just wasn't satisfied. The purse didn't matter that much. I wanted the title to be mine. Whoever won the decider would be The Guv'nor and that's what I wanted above all else. I also wanted Shaw again. I wanted him dead at my feet on the canvas. Well, not literally dead. I wanted to smash him to bits and show him and everybody else what it's like to come up against Lenny McLean. Knocking Roy through the ropes was a technical win but I wanted him in the ring and hurt the next time my hand went up.'

After the fight, Roy Shaw was also keen to have a third and final fight with Lenny. He even challenged Lenny during one of Garry Bushell's TV chat shows in front of millions of viewers. But it never happened; there was no third fight, no decider.

After Lenny McLean's early death, Roy Shaw was magnanimous towards the man who wanted to 'kill' him in the ring.

Roy said, 'Lenny McLean took my title away from

me, took it to the grave. I wouldn't take anything away from him – he won the title fair and square.'

At the end of his autobiography, Lenny wrote, 'Some days get imprinted on your mind more than others. Meeting my wife Val ... the births of my James and Kelly ... and beating Roy Shaw.'

Roy added, 'To me, Lenny was just one in a long line of men I fought throughout my life. No more, no less. So when I read his book, I was touched by his words. I never knew that beating me meant so much to him, so perhaps it was only right that he died still holding the title of The Guv'nor.'

CHAPTER 5

The first prize fight ever recorded took place in 1184 BC and it was a fight to the death.

One of the fighters was a giant of a man named Epeus, the son of the Greek king Epei; the other was Euryalus, a valiant Greek prince who had fought in the Trojan war as a captain in command of 80 ships of war.

Both men wore the dreaded 'caestus' – the world's first knuckle-duster – on their hands, formidable gauntlets made from thongs of raw hide knotted together. The gauntlets had four holes for the fingers and the thumb closed round the outer edge of the gauntlet. The armoured gauntlet was then tied by thongs around the wrist. Beneath the gauntlets, thick woollen gloves were worn.

The two royal warriors were fighting for a fabulous

prize, a 6ft-high, massive, round, solid gold goblet worth a fortune.

The fight was described by Homer, the renowned Greek writer, in an epic poem. The two men faced each other before a great cheering crowd and circled each other with their iron hands held high above their heads, ready to strike whenever an opportunity presented itself. They feinted left and right, darted towards each other and retreated, both trying to find an opening to strike a violent blow.

Unable to find an opening, they approached one another and began to trade blows, hitting each other with their iron fists on the arms and body. Within minutes, their bodies were covered in blood as the gauntlets cut deep gashes in their flesh. Blows were aimed at the head and some got through, causing gashes which removed the skin and the flesh from the face, exposing the teeth and the jaw bone. The blood poured down their bodies in streams, but still the men fought on while the thousands watching the great spectacle cheered on their favourite to move in for the kill.

Exhausted and bleeding profusely, Euryalus dropped his guard and Epeus – 6ft 6in tall – stepped in and brought both his hands down, hitting Euryalus a tremendous blow across the face, so that he fell and lay motionless on the ground.

Homer described how Euryalus's friends dragged him unconscious from the arena, his feet dragging through the dust, his head hanging down, his mouth, nostrils and ears pouring blood.

So dangerous and deadly were the caestus gauntlets

that later fighters wore a head guard to protect themselves against the ferocious blows that could quite easily kill a man. The head guards were made from thickly-quilted bull-hide to dull the blows. The outside was studded with knobs of iron. The head guards were close-fitting like a modern rugby skull cap.

In both the Greek and Roman cultures, the practice of what they called 'pugilism' was considered essential in the education of their youth to 'strengthen the body, end all fear and infuse courage into the boy's character'.

In Britain, both in Roman times and the Middle Ages, boxing was never practised, the rich preferring jousting and fencing, the poor fighting with sandbags and the quarter-staff.

Though the Greeks introduced boxing to the world 3,000 years ago, it was the English – using bare fists – who are credited with inventing bare-knuckle boxing as the ultimate form of duelling. The Greeks used boxing as a discipline, to teach youngsters; as an event, in the Olympic games; and as an art, in the training and practice necessary to make a good fighter.

The English saw a man's fists as the greatest symbol of personal courage. Those Englishmen who championed bare-knuckle boxing despised the French for duelling with swords, the Italians for using the stiletto knife, the Spaniards for using a dagger, the Germans for the sabre, the Americans for using the revolver and the Indians for the bowie knife.

Fighting with naked fists was seen by the English as the practice of cool courage, fair combat, skill and endurance that enhanced the character of Englishmen above all other races and nationalities.

Prize-fighting in Britain developed in the early eighteenth century around the same time as cock-fighting became a national sport. Cock-fighting and prize-fighting were considered to have similar attributes, in which the combatants were admired for their fierce courage, steady nerve, strength and skill. Prize-fighting was also seen as akin to dog-fighting and bear-baiting because all these sports attracted large numbers of people who enjoyed the cruelty and brutality. And the sports were promoted primarily for the purpose of gambling.

The stake money attracted the fighters to take part, but it was the side-stakes, the betting around the ring, that dictated rules should be drawn up before each fight to which all fighters had to agree. Most people believe that prize-fighting would never have become such a popular nationwide sport in Britain if there had been no gambling or stake money.

In around 1750, gambling and drinking were the two passions of English life and both could be enjoyed by young and old, males and females, in the local inn. Unbelievably, it was often in the local pub that urban workers were paid their wages each week and many would end the day going home broke having drunk and gambled away their meagre pay.

Gambling was the reason why parliament declared prize-fighting illegal in 1750, not because of the brutality or danger to life and limb but because the workers were gambling and drinking away all their money.

The government of the day tried to ban prize-fighting altogether, using the same arguments as people do today; that it made men violent, encouraged aggressive behaviour, promoted cruelty and glorified barbarism.

Supporters of prize-fighting argued that the sport taught respect and praised courage, promoted fitness and strength in young men, and did not encourage violence but channelled a man's natural aggression.

Despite the government's attempts to stamp out prize-fighting or boxing of any form, the sport did not die but simply went underground, with the fighters' stake money provided by rich patrons who loved the fight game and, more importantly, the side-betting. When people were earning only a few shillings working a 60-hour week, the stake money for the major fights could be as high as £70, equivalent to five years' wages for a labourer.

One hundred years later, stakes for major fights varied between £100 and £1,000, but these were extraordinary fights between the most celebrated champions. A stake of £50 was usual for high-profile fights, but many fights were arranged for much less. And, as today, the winner took the entire purse, the loser nothing.

England's first ever prize-fighting champion was a man named James Fig from Thame in Oxfordshire, who, in 1719, became known as the Father of the Ring after defeating all-comers. He later set up Britain's first gymnasium – Fig's Ampitheatre in London's Tottenham Court Road – where he trained many boxers and fighters. But most of his fights took place using cudgels – short, heavy sticks – with which they would beat each other over every part of the body, including the head.

Some of his opponents actually died in the ring, but there are no details of individual fights. Fig held the crown as undisputed champion until 1734.

In 1723, King George I, a keen fan of prize-fighting, ordered a ring to be set up in Hyde Park, encircled by a fence, which lasted for 100 years until the government ordered it to be closed down. Indeed, even today, a circle of younger trees near Grosvenor Gate can still be seen marking the outline of the original ring.

One of the first recorded details of a prize fight in England was between a tall, strong Englishman by the name of Bob Whitaker and a giant of a man, described as a Goliath, who was simply named 'The Venetian' because he came from Venice. They fought in Fig's Ampitheatre in 1733.

The record states that the fight was held on a stage erected some 10ft above the ground so everyone in the crowd could see. The size of the Venetian was massive and his arms were long, strong and muscular. By comparison, Whitaker did not seem so big. Both men were armed with cudgels.

As Whitaker approached the Venetian, he was felled by a massive blow to the side of the head, knocking him clear off the stage.

Whitaker hauled himself back on stage and, realising his mistake, ducked underneath the Venetian's club and hit him full in the balls with his cudgel. The Venetian had never before been caught off guard like this and fell to his knees, providing Whitaker with a chance to smash his skull before the giant could get to his feet.

The Venetian managed to stagger to his feet and

refused to fight on, complaining that such blows were 'rude and unmannerly'. Of course, Whitaker was declared the winner.

As a result, Whitaker was challenged by one Nathaniel Peartree, an admirable boxer who concentrated on attacking his opponent's face, not his body. In this fight, only fists were used.

For six minutes, Whitaker was master of the ring, hitting Peartree at will. But Peartree kept hitting Whitaker's eyes, trying to gouge them out with his fingers to blind him. His cunning worked brilliantly and, a minute later, Whitaker was at Peartree's mercy walking around the ring unable to see anything. His eyes had been so badly mangled and thumped he had been blinded.

Whitaker stood in the ring and shouted, 'Damn me, I'm not beat; but I can't fight on 'cos I can't see my man.'

It was during the 1730s that prize-fighting in Britain became more like today's boxing. Cudgels and sticks were banned by agreement between the boxers and only bare fists were permitted. Of course, this produced much longer and more exhausting fights and, in fact, far greater damage to the fighters. When cudgels were used, one or two blows would usually end a fight. From the 1730s onwards, prize-fighting became a much larger spectator sport, for the English loved to see two strong, powerful men knock shit out of each other until one dropped, exhausted, unconsciousness or dead. In most of these fights, the two opponents would stand face-to-face, toe-to-toe and slug it out, hammering away at each other with little or no attempt at defending themselves. As a result, it was usually the more powerful man who won the day. But these fights caused much blood to be spilled, many broken noses and jaws and most fighters could barely see at the end of their fight because of the number of blows aimed at the eyes.

One of the greatest of all English champions was a man by the name of Jack Broughton who reigned supreme against all-comers for 16 years from 1734 to 1750. He was also the founder of self-defence and the first boxer to use his feet rather than stand and belt his opponent as hard as he could. As a result of his footwork, Broughton was hardly ever hit by his opponents and many a stronger, more powerful man lost through sheer exhaustion trying to catch the fleet-of-foot champion.

One of the greatest bare-knuckle fights of all time took place at Banbury, Oxfordshire, in October 1789, between the then champion Tom Johnson, a native of Derby who worked as a corn porter on the Thames, and Isaac Perrins, a 6ft 6in man-mountain who weighed 17 stone and possessed great strength and a ferocious punch .

Johnson was a well-built man, 5ft 9in tall and weighing 14 stone. He was renowned for being cool under pressure and remarkably intelligent. He often out-witted his many opponents by watching them fight against others and working out the best method of attack to guarantee victory. But Perrins was also an intelligent man, worked as a foreman at a Birmingham factory where he was admired by his bosses and praised by the workers under him.

The fight took place on a turfed stage 24ft square

and 5ft above ground level so all the spectators had a good view. With Johnson's stooped style of boxing and Perrins's upright stance, there seemed little chance of a Johnson victory.

An account of the fight reported how, for five minutes, the two bruisers circled each other expectantly before the first blow was struck. Perrins made the first attack but Johnson side-stepped and smashed Perrins in the head, knocking him to the floor.

Johnson began dancing around the huge Perrins, throwing out occasional punches and Perrins could not get within range to land a punch, annoying and irritating the giant. Perrins threw caution to the wind and doggedly followed Johnson round the ring taking many punches before being able to land one himself. But once his thunderous fist hit Johnson, the smaller man went down.

The fight continued in this way with Johnson dancing around and Perrins doggedly following him, not caring how many punches he received. But whenever the bigger man hit his opponent, he knocked him to the floor.

Johnson began to suffer from this punishment and his face became a mass of blood, his lips and nose split open. Then Johnson went on the offensive and hit Perrins above the left eye, cutting the eyebrow and closing the eye completely.

Perrins replied by concentrating on Johnson's eyes and he, too, landed one great punch closing Johnson's right eye. But Johnson's speed and agility helped him to parry one punch from the giant and land a crashing fist on his nose, splitting it in two so that the flesh hung down his cheeks and the blood flowed freely.

In round 41 of the fight, an exhausted Perrins struck Johnson over his other eye so that Johnson could hardly see. And then, without a punch being thrown, Johnson fell to the floor on one knee, exhausted.

Perrins and his corner claimed victory, but the umpires decided the rest was allowable because Johnson got back on his feet.

Unable to strike a decisive blow, Perrins began to copy Johnson's mode of attack, dancing around, throwing the occasional punch. But this totally exhausted the huge man and he was clearly out of breath, hardly able to move around the ring.

So Perrins began to fight low, trying to hit Johnson's testicles whenever he came into range.

But Johnson found his second breath and, being the fitter man, taunted the giant Perrins who tried desperately to land heavy blows in a bid to end the fight quickly. Delivering one such blow, Perrins missed and fell.

As Perrins was slowly falling to the floor, Johnson leapt forward and hit him full in the face. The effort exhausted him and he, too, fell to the floor. But he recovered more quickly and Johnson now seemed to hit Perrins whenever he tried.

In round 62, after one-and-a-quarter hours of fighting, Johnson gathered all his strength for one final, colossal blow, and struck Perrins in the centre of his face, knocking him out cold. Perrins fell backwards unconscious and crashed on his back to the floor of the stage. That was the end.

The fight was considered to have been the toughest and greatest duel ever fought in the history of eighteenth-century bare-knuckle boxing. It was officially described as 'fair, hard boxing'.

One of the longest fights in the history of bare-knuckle boxing took place in 1790 when 'Big Ben' (whose real name was Benjamin Brain, a coal miner) and Hill Hooper, known as 'Tinman', went 180 rounds together in a celebrated fight at Newbury in Berkshire.

The contest turned into a marathon because Tinman refused to stand and trade punches. After receiving one horrendous punch from Big Ben which sent him flying, he kept his distance. Instead of throwing punches, he kept throwing insults at his opponent and running around the ring, keeping as far away from Big Ben as possible. In the end, Big Ben just stood in the centre of the ring and lashed out whenever Tinman came close enough. Occasionally, the Tinman did land a pathetic punch on his opponent, but for the most part he just kept walking around him. As night fell, the umpires declared the contest a draw but Big Ben had not received one painful punch.

Time-keeping was not restricted to the duration of the round but only the half-minute interval. When the bell sounded at the end of the interval, both boxers had to walk to the centre of the ring – called the scratch – ready to join battle. If a fighter was unable 'to come to the scratch' his opponent was declared the winner.

The rounds lasted until a man, or indeed both men, were knocked or thrown off their feet. In some respects, prize-fighting was a mixture of boxing and wrestling because it was quite legitimate for a fighter to throw his man so he fell on his back, thus ending a round. A round could, therefore, last a matter of seconds or much, much longer. The fact that many fights lasted 50 rounds does not in itself reveal the length of time over which it was contested. It is impossible to state the average length of a fight, but most observers believed that about 30 rounds would generally last one hour. Some fights fought over 200 rounds or more lasted only four hours. In other fights, one round might last more than 20 minutes.

However, when two top boxers fought for substantial prize money, most rounds only lasted about two minutes because of the severity of the punches and the effect they had on the fighters.

In the history of bare-knuckle boxing, one man's name has always stood out. Daniel Mendoza, an educated Jew from Whitechapel in London, became one of the most elegant and scientific boxers of all time. Born in 1763, his first recorded fight was against Harry the Coalheaver in 1784 when he was just 21. He polished off Harry in just 40 minutes.

Mendoza was not very well built or heavy, but he was quick and agile. He would deliver a flurry of punches to his opponent when, in those days, most boxers concentrated on trying to deliver one massive, killer punch. He was only 5ft 7in tall and about 13 stone, but he had strong arms and he also had remarkable spirit, determination and courage.

Mendoza's forefathers included a physician who had served a king of Spain, another who had sailed with Christopher Columbus and a third who had commanded a cavalry regiment in the wars of Philip II of Spain. Daniel Mendoza was also dignified, graceful and handsome.

Mendoza became a boxer by accident. At the age of 16, he was working for a tea dealer in Mincing Lane, London, when a big, bulky porter delivered a consignment of tea. Mendoza's old employer gave him one penny – the customary tip – but the porter grabbed him and threatened to thump him if he did not give him sixpence.

Mendoza, then a stripling of a lad, stepped in, seized the bully's upraised arm and threatened to thrash him 'for his insolence'.

The porter roared with laughter. 'I could chew you up and spit you out,' he said.

Young Mendoza ignored the remark, took off his coat and walked out into Mincing Lane preparing to fight the man. The bully had to accept the challenge.

When those outside realised a fight was about to take place, a couple of hundred men gathered round. It seemed ridiculous. Here was a slight, young schoolboy attempting to tackle a 6ft 2in tall, 17-stone porter. Someone ran off to call the police to stop the fight. They needn't have bothered. Young Mendoza tore into the bully with a flurry of fast, accurate, cutting punches, his knuckles breaking open the man's face. But two huge punches from the porter sent Mendoza crashing to the ground and those watching tried to end the fight before he suffered more punishment.

Mendoza would have none of it and returned to the fray. In the next 30 minutes, Mendoza smashed the man to the ground a dozen times with ferocious punching. Mendoza had won his first fight.

One man watching that extraordinary fight was Richard Humphries, a rich dandy who ran his own boxing gymnasium in London. He also happened to be one of the best boxers of his day. On his return to his gymnasium he proclaimed, 'I have just seen the future champion of England.'

Humphries decided to take young Mendoza under his wing and teach him all the skills of bare-knuckle boxing. Humphries took him to a mansion in Epping Forest which had been loaned to him by a rich merchant. Mendoza recalled what he found there.

'The house was full of young women and the servants half-tipsy, most of them needing a good wash.

'Almost immediately, young women began pulling me this way and that, enticing me to bedrooms. I quickly realised I was in a rather grand brothel.'

Urged to relax and enjoy himself by his trainer, Mendoza agreed to stay on and, for one week, he went wild, indulging himself with 20 or so young women in every kind of sexual activity. He would spend most of the day surrounded by naked young women who would take turns to have sex with the fit, strong, young boxer with the muscular body and remarkable stamina. At night, he would sleep with three or four of the women.

Later, his host Humphries would tell how fights had broken out among the young harlots who were so keen to have sex with him that they actually resorted to fighting and punching each other in their bid to lay him. Apparently, young Mendoza took all this in his stride, for it was the first time in his life that he had ever been in such a situation where he could have sex with as many women as he wanted, whenever he wanted.

In the evening, dinner parties – which were more like wild orgies – would take place for a few of Humphries' select friends who were served their wine and their food by the naked girls who would happily carry out whatever sexual practices the guests required. Apparently, Mendoza, who had led a sheltered life, was shocked by some of the demands, which included sado-masochistic whipping and bondage in full view of all the guests, many of whom were hopelessly drunk.

Mendoza, however, knew that he had to prepare for a scheduled fight and he realised that if he stayed drinking and wenching all day and all night he would hardly be able to crawl into the boxing ring, let alone fight. He decided to leave the house and the non-stop debauchery, much to the anger of Humphries who from that day on began a vicious vendetta against Mendoza which was to last for decades.

It was shortly after this week-long orgy that Daniel Mendoza was privileged to be introduced to the young Prince Frederick George, who was then in his twenties and a man keen on bare-knuckle fighting and a full and varied sex life, which included whores and harlots as well as ladies he found at court. Later, Frederick George would become Prince Regent and he reigned as King George IV from 1820 to 1830.

The young Prince George was then a great gambler and a keen supporter of young Daniel Mendoza and would wager vast amounts of money on the young boxer. Of course, one of the reasons Prince George was so taken by Daniel was the fact that he won small fortunes whenever Mendoza entered the boxing ring.

Mendoza met the Prince minutes before stepping into the ring – a stage set high above the crowd – for a spectacular fight attended by tens of thousands of people who flocked to Barnet to see him fight against Mister Martin, the Butcher from Bath who was built like a bulldog, squat and square.

A report of the fight stated that, after a few minutes of the Butcher charging at Mendoza like a bull, snorting and swinging his fists wildly, Mendoza waited for a few seconds and then hit the Butcher with his left sending him sprawling. As he was about to fall from the stage, someone pushed him back on against all the rules.

In the following round, a lumbering Martin was met by a swift, savage blow to the face which smashed his nose to a pulp. Mendoza pivoted hard on his heel and drove for the heart. The big Butcher's ruddy face went bloodless and pale like a corpse's. He doubled up in pain, his mouth gaping open, and the young Mendoza brought his fist crashing against the heavy jowl. The Butcher's mouth snapped like a steel trap and he fell to the floor, his teeth spilling out of his mouth.

The Butcher's corner managed to get the champion back into the ring but, once again, Mendoza hit him square between the eyes with a thunderous right. The Butcher nearly fell from the stage, only to be rescued again by the same helper. This time, Mendoza had had enough. He went over to the man and with one crashing fist sent him flying from the stage into the milling mob that was screaming and shouting by the ringside.

Once more, the Butcher staggered to his feet and this time Mendoza delivered the *coup de grace* with a right to the jaw.

The Prince of Wales called for Mendoza who had just made him a few thousand pounds and shook him by the hand.

'Mendoza,' the Prince said, 'I see no reason at all why you should not be Champion of England within a year.'

Proud and honoured, Mendoza replied, 'Your Royal Highness is more than generous. I am deeply moved.'

But what pleased Mendoza that day was not only his victory against a far more powerful opponent, but that many of his friends and relatives from East London had come to see the fight and bet their wages on his victory. Now, the Cockneys of London not only had a champion bare-knuckle boxer but someone whom the Prince of Wales saluted as a champion and a friend. They also had some winnings in their pockets.

Mendoza would have three fights against his arch-rival Humphries which were among the most vicious ever recorded in the history of prize-fighting. Humphries was jealous and full of hate for the man he insultingly called 'The Jew'. In the first fight, Mendoza slipped, twisting his ankle, but that didn't stop Humphries from mercilessly hammering Mendoza who was unable to stand.

For 12 months, Mendoza was unable to fight as his ankle slowly healed, during which time he earned no money and his enemy Humphries declared him a coward in a newspaper article. That article was the spur Mendoza needed and he returned immediately to training. Once again, his followers flocked to see him training and began placing their bets. They had lost their shirts on Mendoza's first fight with Humphries but they still backed their man.

Their second bout at Stilton in Huntingdonshire began at one in the afternoon one May Day with the scent of wet grass and lilac in the air. Three thousand men had packed into a walled garden of a gentleman's country estate.

In an account of the fight, we read that they cautiously sparred with one another, as watchful as big cats. For the first few rounds, they rotated on the green turf then Humphries jumped in and snaked a left towards Mendoza's head, followed by a swift right to the body. Mendoza stopped the blows easily.

Then suddenly Mendoza was on the offensive. He hammered a lightning barrage of blows at his opponent's head and body, then, with a short, sharp right to the jaw, he knocked Humphries clean off his feet.

Humphries winced and grinned. Mockingly he praised Mendoza for the punch.

Humphries' grin infuriated Mendoza who tore into his arch enemy and smashed one savage blow into Humphries' face, then another, then another. Blood streamed from the smashed nose and lips of his former boxing master.

Somehow, Humphries battled on desperately. He was taking a bad hiding, especially as he had boasted before the fight that he would thrash the Jew until he crawled for mercy. But Mendoza battled on, his fists and forearms now covered in Humphries's blood.

Mendoza hit his man to the jaw; now to the ribs; then more jabs to the ribs, the jaw, the heart. Then, as

Humphries blundered about in the arena receiving dozens of blows from Mendoza's rock-hard knuckles which tore into his body, he realised the end was near. Humphries gave up the fight, dropping to the ground.

In the Articles of Agreement drawn up between the two men before the fight, the man who dropped to the ground without receiving a punch forfeited the fight. Pandemonium broke out as Humphries's corner claimed the fight was a draw and demanded another fight at some time in the future. The screaming fans yelled their defiance, rightly claiming Mendoza to have won fair and square.

As the noise and mayhem raged, Humphries recovered, got to his feet and challenged Mendoza to a future fight.

'Very well then, Mister Humphries,' shouted Mendoza and charged out of his corner, smashing Humphries on the side of the head and knocking him to the ground once more. Humphries recovered again and attempted to continue the fight, but was floored by a ferocious right to the body. Down he went a third time. Humphries showed remarkable courage, continuing to stagger to his feet time after time, only to be smashed down again by ferocious punching from Mendoza. The crowd loved it, cheering every time Mendoza battered his man into submission. Finally, after an hour of fighting, Humphries fell unconscious to the ground and was carried away, inert as a coffin.

A year later, the two champions met for the third and last time in September 1790 at Doncaster, a day after the St Leger had run. Tickets for the fight, held at the Rose and Crown on the River Don, were priced at half-a-guinea, although tickets changed hands for ten guineas (equivalent to £100 today) when the average man's weekly wage was a few shillings a week.

A huge crowd in excess of 5,000 men turned up to watch the grudge match of the century. The first round went to the eager Humphries who felled Mendoza with a right below the belt, in the pit of his stomach. (There were no rules against low punches.)

In the second round, the two men exchanged several blows before Humphries grabbed his smaller, lighter opponent and attempted to hurl him bodily to the ground. For five long minutes the two men held each other in a vice-like grip, their eyes full of hate just a few inches from the other. Finally, both men fell together to the boards and had to be prised apart by their seconds.

Humphries opened the third round believing he had the advantage, striding after Mendoza and throwing punches into his face. Then, suddenly, Daniel Mendoza stood still as a rock, took one more punch and then counter-attacked ferociously. Left! Right! Left! Left! Savagely, he unleashed a lightning attack and every blow thudded sickeningly into Humphries's face. Punch after punch drove Humphries around the ring. Within two minutes, his right eye was closed, his left eye was streaming blood and he could barely see Mendoza's flying fists before another thunderous blow shook him to the core. The side of his nose was split as cleanly as if it had been slashed by a razor and the blood was running into his mouth and covering his chest.

Humphries was a beaten and battered man unable to defend himself and Mendoza finally took pity on him,

Lenny psyches himself up before a fight.

Above: The Guv'nor prepares to do battle and, *below*, heading into the ring.

Roy 'Pretty Boy' Shaw gets set to make ugly work of an opponent.

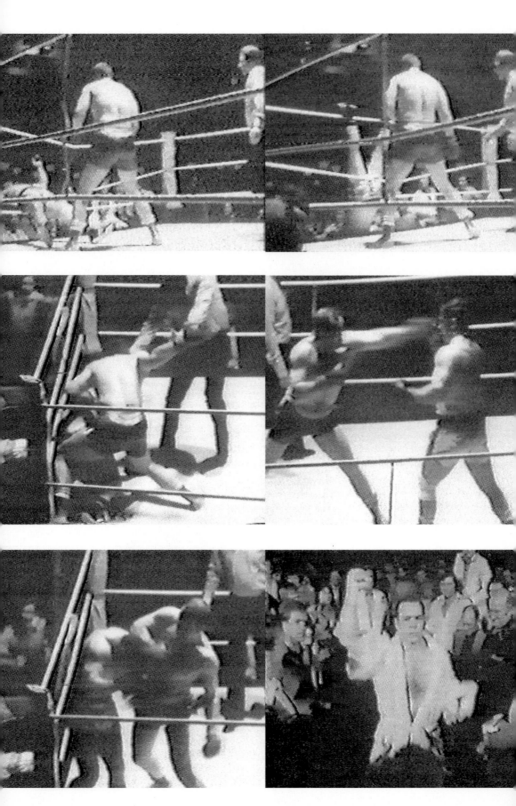

Rare and breathtaking footage of Lenny and Roy in the ring together.

Roy Shaw with Joe Pyle (*left*) and Alex Steen.

Above: Roy Shaw and Donny 'The Bull' Adams square up.

Below: Nosher Powell in the ring with Laurence Harvey.

BOXING

at the

RAINBOW THEATRE
FINSBURY PARK LONDON

on

11th September 1978

In aid of CHILDRENS MUSCULAR DYSTROPHY & AUTISTIC CHILDREN

Featuring a 10 x 3m

CLOSE ENCOUNTER FOR A THIRD TIME for the UNOFFICIAL

HEAVYWEIGHT CHAMPIONSHIP of GREAT BRITAIN

Lennie 'Boy' McLean
THE COOLEST DADDY OF THEM ALL

Roy 'Pretty Boy' Shaw
WILL THE MEAN MACHINE REGAIN THE TITLE

Steve 'Columbo' Richards	Tommy Adams	John McDade
v	v	v
Steve Armstrong	Micky May	Danny Woods

Ralph Harris	Terry Scrutton	Micky Davison
v	v	v
Danny Chippendale	John Ricky	To be announced

Doors open at 7.00 p.m.   Boxing commences 8.00 p.m.

Tickets: £12.50 £10.00 £7.50 £5.00 £2.50

AVAILABLE FROM

C. PINI 01 837 6891

DIXIE DEAN 01 253 8072

RAINBOW BOX OFFICE

HENRY BROWN 01 739 7582

The poster advertising the third and final fight between Roy and Lenny.

only jabbing at him gently, urging him to end the fight before he took any more punishment. Finally, Humphries dropped to the floor a broken man, and his friends picked him up and carried him away on their shoulders like a dying soldier from the battlefield.

As a result, Humphries, who had once been the greatest bare-knuckle fighter in England, retired forever from the ring and Mendoza, now 26, was hailed as the new champion.

There were other such champions arriving on the scene around this time, young men who, through their speed and agility, came to knock hell out of big, tough, strong older champions who relied only on brute strength and a massive punch. Young Jim Belcher was one such youngster who, at the age of 16, and still a stripling, stepped into the ring against Bob Britton, the huge heavyweight champion of the West Country.

The odds had been 4–1 against Jim Belcher still standing after 15 minutes in the ring. Thirty minutes into the fight, the battered hulk of Bob Britton just managed to stagger around the ring, weak as a child, half-blinded, with a face so bloody it looked as if it had been gashed by a butcher's knife. He had been given a lesson in boxing that he would never forget. The age of modern, speedy, agile boxers had arrived. It was 1798.

After Mendoza, Jim Belcher was considered one of the greatest of all boxers. He would dispatch fine champions, who boasted of many victories, within ten minutes of entering the ring, by the speed and accuracy of his punches which cut his opponents' faces to bloody ribbons and closed their eyes as his bare knuckles hit deep in the eye sockets. He earned a small fortune with his fists, and he was hardly ever hit because of his side-stepping, weaving and swaying and the speed of his feet. He soon could afford to live in great style in a large house not far from Aldgate pump, employing man-servants and maids, and dressing like a fashionable dandy. The public loved his style and cheered him to the heavens whenever he entered the ring. Young Jim Belcher, of course, had helped line the pockets of his admirers who won good wagers backing the stripling on his way to the top.

And then there was 'Pretty Boy' George Horton, a butcher's boy from Bristol, who was cursed with curly blond hair and the pretty-pretty looks of a delicate girl. By the age of 12, George Horton hated his pretty face and cherubic lips, and yearned to have buck teeth, a squint and a menacing look.

So young George devised a plan. Whenever he was teased about his 'pretty good looks', he would challenge the lad to a fight. And the bigger the bully, the better. The more punishment he took, the happier he became and would seek out fights with stronger, older boys who would bash his face to a pulp. But his plan didn't work.

By the age of 20, young women would go weak at the knees at the sight of the Bristol lad whom some women described as the most handsome and beautiful man in the world. As a result of his constant fights and bare-knuckle bouts in the ring, George had, by accident, developed the muscles and body of a Roman gladiator.

In his bid to alter his appearance, George went looking for trouble. He began to seduce other men's wives in public in the hope that the husbands would, in sheer rage, find strength enough to flatten his nose. He visited seamen's taverns and drank other people's beer so that they would knock hell out of him. When he received such batterings, he would go home with a split nose, a black eye or a bleeding mouth but within a matter of days the injuries would have healed and he would be as handsome as ever.

One day, the butcher's boy told a well-known sea captain to take away his carcass of beef because it was old and rotten. The Captain, Ned Weston, was a hulk of a man well known as a brawler in sea ports around southern Britain. He also had the dubious reputation of having killed a man in Belfast with one punch.

Ned Weston simply laughed at the pretty boy who challenged him to a fight over the carcass of rotten meat. But George Horton wasn't kidding. He wanted to teach the brash, bully of a sea captain a lesson, for trying to sell him old meat. Finally, George decided he would have to give the captain a sharp right to the jaw to show him he meant business. It worked, angering Weston, who began to set about the boy.

This time, however, young George was in a fury and he retaliated hard and fast. George hit the 17-stone captain exactly 8 times in 60 seconds, the final punch landing on the point of the chin, knocking him out cold. News of the extraordinary victory reverberated around Bristol and George Horton's phenomenal career began.

Finally, however, George met the man who would eventually thrash him and, more importantly, someone who had the power to disfigure the beautiful face that George so hated. Tom Cribb was a massive bare-knuckle boxer with bulging, muscular shoulders and arms, and had a punch like a donkey's kick. The more he punished the face and the body of 'Pretty' George Horton, the more George staggered to his feet to take yet more punishment. Young George's nose was smashed repeatedly by the bare-knuckle fists of Tom Cribb until his nose, broken in several places, resembled a squashed tomato. Showing extraordinary courage, George got to his feet for the last round, staggering helplessly around the ring, his eyes almost closed, his ears bleeding, his lips broken open and his front teeth knocked out.

Eventually, Lord Byron ordered George's corner to 'Throw in the sponge, for God's sake, before the poor beggar needs a coffin.'

Four weeks after that fight, George checked the mirror and saw before him a flattened, twisted nose, thickened ears and a crooked smile in a scarred mouth in which several teeth were missing. George went home to Bristol a happy man and settled down peacefully to become a prosperous, ugly, unremarkable butcher. But, apparently, he always had a smile on his face.

In 1804, the first black man to make his mark in the boxing world arrived in England from America in search of the World Boxing title. Young Tom Molyneux – or Black Tom, as he was called – a Negro slave working on a cotton plantation in Richmond, Virginia, had won his freedom in a bare-knuckle contest in which he had destroyed his black opponent. He had teamed up with a wily white man named Sailor Mason, who ran a travelling boxing booth. Mason described Black Tom as follows: 'A huge black man with ebony skin, the strength of an ox, bullock-like shoulders, fists like elephants' feet and thighs like stumps of trees.'

Together, Sailor Mason and Black Tom toured America beating all-comers who dared to enter the ring, and together they earned lots of money which Sailor Mason mainly spent on booze. He even persuaded Black Tom to join him in drinking bouts. Five years later, Sailor Mason decided it was time for Black Tom to travel to England to fight for the World Championship of Boxing. He was convinced that no man on earth could beat his Black Tom.

Finally, a fight for the World Championship was agreed after Black Tom destroyed every bare-knuckle fighter who dared to enter the ring to fight him. The Corinthians, the London sporting club who championed boxing matches, demanded that Tom Cribb, the English champion, must face Black Tom. The contest, if that is how it can be described, took place in December 1810.

At the end of the twenty-eighth round, Tom Cribb lay at Black Tom's feet lifeless, totally unconscious for a full half-minute. Not only had Tom Cribb been destroyed, so had England's reputation as the boxing capital of the world.

So angry and distraught were the thousands of fight fans who had watched the epic fight that they yelled their disapproval at the outcome, refusing to accept that a negro from America was now Champion of England and Champion of the World. Tom Cribb's seconds claimed that Black Tom had fought with bullets in his hands. It was, of course, totally untrue and Black

Tom proved it by opening his hands to let everyone see that the accusation was false. But the crowd refused to listen. Tom Cribb was declared the winner. Poor Black Tom knew he had won and knew he had been cheated. All he could do was wait for another chance to prove he was the World Champion.

But Black Tom, by nature a quiet, gentle person, had other problems. The young girls of Somerset took a fancy to this magnificent specimen of manhood much to the anger and bitterness of the local youths. One night, as he took his evening walk, 20 or so young men, some with knuckle-dusters, ambushed the gentle giant, determined to thrash him so badly he would leave the village of Winfold where he was living at the time. It was a one-sided fight; Black Tom destroyed 12 of the young men, knocking them unconscious, before the rest turned and fled.

Sailor Mason and Black Tom took to the road again and earned fortunes from fights across England with Black Tom taking on three or four fighters at a time. But he was also drinking heavily for, at heart, he was now dreadfully unhappy, feeling like a hunted beast whom everyone wanted to destroy. In September 1811, another fight was organised between a strong, healthy, athletic Tom Cribb and a bloated, overweight, miserable Black Tom. The black contender put up a gallant fight but he was so slow and cumbersome around the ring that Tom Cribb had little difficulty in landing punches whenever he wanted. In the end, Black Tom lay on the ground helpless, his jaw broken, his spirit finally destroyed.

From Thomas Cribb onwards, there were, of course,

a succession of champions, amongst them some courageous and talented bare-knuckle fighters. But those remembered for their extraordinary prowess were few and far between.

There was George Cooper, a native of Stone in Staffordshire, who had the ability to take heavy punishment before counter-attacking strongly and flooring his opponent who seemed dazed and mesmerised by Cooper's ferocious punching. Indeed, Cooper's skill became legendary and champion boxers found themselves out-boxed and out-witted by Cooper's speed and accuracy. Many opponents appeared to be lumbering novices when they faced Cooper, a small man standing only 5ft 8in tall and weighing only 12 stone. He was so quick they hardly ever managed to hit him, while his flashing fists kept landing on target until his opponents' faces were a mass of bleeding pulp.

Another lightweight who succeeded in damaging much heavier and stronger boxers was Jack Randall, an Irish lad who was only 10st 6lb and 5ft 6in tall. Randall began his boxing career at the beginning of the nineteenth century when aged only 14 and caught the imagination of the boxing world with his brilliant style which seemed to flummox and confuse his opponents.

Randall would often finish a fight in a matter of a few rounds and his opponent would usually be left with severe cuts and bruises to the face as well as having endured a severe thumping in the pit of his stomach. But Randall would barely have a single mark on his face. In those days of bare-knuckle boxing, it was extraordinary for a man to escape any injury or visible marks at the end of a contest unless he showed brilliant technique in the art of defence.

One of Randall's greatest conquests, for which he was praised for elevating prize-fighting to the highest standard, was against a man named Belasco, considered the greatest exponent of the art of in-fighting. The fight took place at Shepperton in 1817 with the odds virtually even. The match was a classic with both boxers treating each other with great respect for the first few rounds.

From the third round onwards, however, the crowd of several thousand were cheering themselves hoarse as the two men punched and counter-punched with great ferocity, sometimes hitting the face, at other times having their shots parried. But Randall began to get the better of Belasco, repeatedly hitting him in the face with a succession of quick one-twos, until Belasco twice went down under the barrage of punches.

Randall boxed with remarkable precision, seemingly knowing where his next punch would land and where it would do the most damage. After the fight, which Randall won quite easily in the end, the acknowledged boxing experts described the fight as 'one of the the most perfect specimens of boxing ever witnessed'.

It was no wonder that, following this match, Randall was described as being the best boxer the world had ever known.

But, occasionally, Randall fought some very tough opponents. One was Edward Turner, a strong Welshman with a good reputation as a boxer of hardness and quality. It was a remarkable fight which lasted two hours, nineteen minutes and thirty seconds, and the two men fought a total of 34 rounds. Ultimately, Randall was a comfortable winner, but only because he was not put down. Turner could not even drag himself to his feet at the end; his face was a bloody mess, and he had a broken nose and broken teeth. His whole body was covered in his blood and he had to be physically carried from the ring. Randall had taken some punches but his face was barely marked. No one could tell that he had been involved in one of the toughest and longest fights ever undertaken by a champion.

In the eighteenth and nineteenth centuries, the great majority of prize-fighters ended their days as publicans which the local magistrates encouraged because these pubs posed no problem for local police because the former prize-fighter would stop any trouble-makers in their tracks.

In 1750, prize-fighting was declared illegal by an Act of Parliament which pushed the promotion and organisation of fights underground. The venues could not be advertised in advance and no tickets could be sold beforehand. Fortunately, many magistrates simply turned a blind eye to the bouts and the backers, including the aristocracy, continued to support and enjoy the sport.

Pubs remained the centre of prize-fighting for various reasons. In 1803, there were 50,000 inn-keepers in a total population of only nine million people. The publicans were sometimes constables, coal merchants or promoters of friendly societies and thrift clubs. Local clubs met in pubs, many workmen were paid their weekly wages at the local pub and, of course, they were also the centre of village and town life.

Prize-fighters were nearly always given nicknames under which they fought. The idea was taken from the early Middle Ages when knights fought in tournaments using nicknames. The names were sometimes puns, at other times jokes and some fighters took honorary titles.

The great majority of the top fighters gained substantial earnings from their many fights and should have retired rich men compared to the great majority of the population. But there were many, unused to money, who ended their days in poverty, spending all they earned in pubs with so-called mates, gambling on horses and other fights and simply handing too much over to those who worked in their corners, trained them or managed their boxing careers.

Many prize fights were promoted by wealthy patrons who put up the purse for which the boxers fought. Other patrons backed their own man against another fighter and paid their own man a purse whether he won or lost. Most of the leading fighters up to 1814 had their own backer, or backers, who raised the side-stake and supported the fighter when he was in training. Indeed, nearly all cricket matches during those centuries were arranged on the same basis.

The prize-fighters' patrons ranged from royalty down through various members of the aristocracy to businessmen, merchants and publicans. George IV, as Prince of Wales, was probably the keenest backer and he would often be seen at prize fights eagerly cheering on his own boxer. Indeed, at his coronation, George IV engaged 18 of England's top prize-fighters to guard the external avenues leading to Westminster Hall from unauthorised visitors. The boxers, whom he dressed as pages, were the leading prize-fighters of the decade. For the record, they did their job that day perfectly for no uninvited guests managed to gain entry.

In 1814, the Pugilistic Club was formed to take over responsibility for staging prize fights and, as a result, the private patron took a back seat. The Pugilistic Club was formed by a dozen patrons of the fight game. The Club had a Secretary and Treasurer and soon had a membership of 120 subscribers, some subscribing 50 guineas a year, others 10 guineas. The main reason was to stop boxers selling their contests to unauthorised backers.

But prize-fighting was not the only spectator sport to attract the crowds during those centuries. Other sports, actively enjoyed by many men from all walks of life, included racing, cricket, cock-fighting, dog-fighting and bull-baiting, all of which attracted betting. But hunting, fishing and coursing, though popular, attracted no gambling and, as a consequence, no spectators.

CHAPTER 6

Nosher Powell was the ultimate hard man, a force to be reckoned with. As a heavyweight boxing champion or a bare-knuckle fighter, Nosher knew few equals. In 78 professional boxing matches, he was never once knocked out.

He learned to live by two hard rules and kept to them throughout his career in the ring and in his dealings outside the ring with hard men where his fists did the talking.

Nosher decreed, 'The first rule of street fighting is to hit first, and keep hitting. It's nasty, it's messy, but it's essential. While the other guy can still get up, he's dangerous.

'The second rule is to remember a man is either born with a punch or he's not, and no amount of training can teach a man that.'

Nosher's boxing career nearly came to an end when he was 16 years old. He had enjoyed a few fights but he was untrained and would too frequently find himself getting thumped too often and too hard.

One day, he was fooling around with mates in the market when he ran out of the halls and raced slap-bang into the side of a car. He hurtled right through the side window.

Nosher lost consciousness and was rushed to hospital. His right arm had been shattered and his face looked as though he had been cut to pieces and battered. He lay in the hospital for three months but the bad news was that all the tendons in his right hand had been severed and he would never fully regain the muscle tone. His entire right hand was numb and it has stayed numb throughout his life.

However, that numb hand meant he could use it like a club and, more importantly, he would never feel a thing. In the years to come, Nosher used that fist to settle scores and win some fights. He called it his 'Fist of Numbness'.

Like almost every other teenager at that time, Nosher was called up to do his National Service and he was keen to join the Army and see the world. He told the doctor examining him that his right hand was fine. If he had told the truth, he would never have been accepted and might not have become a great boxing champion. He reported for duty at the Queen's Regiment Barracks in Canterbury and, after 12 weeks' basic training, was transferred to the Royal Army Medical Corps.

Within a couple of weeks, Nosher found himself on board a troop ship bound for the Middle East, and the ship's captain 'volunteered' Nosher to fight the heavyweight champion of the Palestine police force who also happened to be on the same ship. It was an unequal contest; Ahmed, the Palestine cop, was fit, highly experienced and weighed 15st 4lb while Nosher was 18, inexperienced and just 12st 9lb.

The entire ship's company turned out for this one-sided fight held on deck, but they did cheer for Nosher.

Later, he recounted what happened. 'Ahmed came out of his corner like Guy the Gorilla, only uglier and oozing menace. I knew that, if that big bastard hit me hard, I would be a goner, so I decided my only chance was to keep moving around the ring.

'Thank God Ahmed was slow and cumbersome and I started prodding his face with my long left arm as his haymakers missed my head by inches. It stayed like that into the third round; Ahmed lumbering about, me ducking and diving.

'Suddenly, I saw an opening and that was the moment to unload my famous Fist of Numbness, smack on his chin. Ahmed stopped dead in his tracks and I swear he was out on his feet before he began to topple. I managed to wallop him four more times before he hit the deck.

'I felt fantastic and the cheers around the entire deck were music to my ears. For the first time in my life, I knew what it was like to be a sporting hero and I loved it.'

His victory at sea, however, meant that Nosher was going to be kept busy, not tending the wounded in battle but fighting for the honour of the regiment in the boxing ring. His Colonel volunteered Nosher to fight the Royal Australian Air Force's heavyweight champion in a boxing match in the grounds of an Egyptian military hospital.

Nosher stopped the Aussie in two rounds.

Nosher said later, 'After that, they brought in blokes against me like an Aunt Sally stall at a fairground. They put 'em up, I knocked 'em down. Simple.'

For no apparent reason, Nosher was transferred to the Para Field Ambulance Unit in Palestine and began boring guard duty but he remembered to keep himself in good physical condition. One day, he saw a stranger in the camp shadow-boxing and, after making enquiries, he found the keen boxer was not only the regimental heavyweight champion but also the Palestine Army Champion!

His Sergeant only laughed at Nosher, telling him he looked more like a college professor than a heavyweight bruiser. Nosher was totally unmarked and even his nose looked as though it had never been hit.

The regimental heavyweight, a Welshman by the name of Bellamy, was only too happy to have someone as a sparring partner and Nosher was taken off guard duty, given extra rations, and began training and sparring with the champ.

One week later, Nosher was given permission by the PTI (Physical Training Instructor) to challenge Bellamy. Nosher knocked out the champion inside a minute. He now became a fully-fledged member of the Medical Corps regimental boxing team. Fights were arranged and Nosher won all of them. In no time, he had become United Services and Imperial Services heavyweight champion, flattening all-comers.

Nosher was selected to be a member of the British Army's team of finest boxers because a challenge had been laid down on behalf of the Egyptian Olympic team by none other than King Farouk, the Egyptian King.

The training of the British Army team was harsh and rigorous. Tough sparring sessions were held every afternoon after arduous training all morning. No head guards were used and the gloves were thin and knobbly, giving little protection. Every punch that landed crunched the knuckles. There were many bloody noses, damaged faces and many a knock-out. To assist recovery, a bucket of cold water was simply thrown over the unconscious boxer. By the time the contest arrived, however, the British Army team were superbly fit, well muscled, and very, very tough.

As heavyweight, Nosher was last on. The other seven British boxers had won their bloody fights. Minutes before Nosher was due in the ring the other seven boxers came to see him with a message.

'Listen, Nosher,' said their spokesman, 'we're just here to wish you luck – and to tell you that if you get beat, we're going to kick seven shades of fucking shit out of you! Understand?'

Nosher's Egyptian opponent was a 17-stone weightlifter, a big lump of a man. Nosher weighed in at 12 stone. After two minutes of sparring Nosher saw an opening and went in with a crashing right cross. It was all over.

To Nosher's consternation, the Army's Commanding Officer, Brigadier-General Gale, put him forward to fight the Egyptian Army's *professional* heavyweight. General Gale told Nosher he had changed his name to Leroy Brown and that he would be paid £30 for the fight, win or lose. At that time, Nosher was earning exactly 75p a week! He grabbed at the chance. Nosher won that eight-round fight on points but he was absolutely knackered at the final bell; he had never boxed for longer than three rounds in his entire life!

But in his 30 fights in Egypt, only one man beat him, a former ABA champion by the name of Andy Gill, who traded punch for punch with Nosher in a ferocious fight. Nosher lost on points but his body had taken one hell of a beating. Nosher was angry with himself for becoming too cocky, not bothering to get super-fit for that fight. He was determined that would never happen again. He went to work, giving himself a punishing regime to make sure that he would be in peak physical condition for a return bout with Gill.

The return was a sell-out; the gymnasium in Port Said, Egypt, was packed to the rafters. Once again, however, Nosher at 12 stone was giving away 3 stone. But Gill looked as though he hadn't trained for this fight and Nosher went to work. It was a blood and guts fight with both boxers standing toe-to-toe in the ring trading punches.

In the second round, Gill was fighting for breath, his nose smashed, the blood trickling down his throat.

In the third round, Nosher saw the opening he wanted and crashed a right into Gill. Nosher was still hitting him as he slid to the canvas, out for the count.

Nosher's final fight in the Army was against the US heavyweight champion of the American Pacific Fleet, a very good boxer who knew after the first round that he could easily defeat Nosher. But he became over-confident, dancing round the ring, showing off to the 5,000 US sailors who came to cheer on their champ. Nosher waited and then struck and the big American went through the ropes like a blob of jelly. The man Nosher beat that day was named Tami Moriella who, two years later, went on to fight the great Joe Louis for the heavyweight championship of the world. Tami lost that fight, too, but it did mean that, by the age of 21, Nosher had taken on a world championship contender – and won.

Back in Civvy Street, Nosher decided to turn pro and went to see Jack Solomons, the boxing promotor with the large figure, flamboyant bow-ties and big cigars. Jack agreed to promote fights for Nosher, and on his first night, Nosher had to face three heavyweights, one after the other. He won all three and a cheque for £500, a small fortune in those days.

Nosher came to a deal with Jack Solomons. He would spar with all the American fighters he brought to Britain and, in return, he would find Nosher a spot on the bill. So Nosher got a sparring fee, and money for the fight.

Sometimes, however, Nosher found himself up against really good boxers, bruisers and fighters. And, sometimes, the going was tough, tougher than he wanted. In one fight, during the early days with Jack Solomons, Nosher and his opponent, hard-hitter Jack Longford, knocked each other down a total of 13 times over 8 rounds. At the finish, both men were black-and-blue with cut eyes, cut noses, cut mouths and their bodies were smothered in blood and sweat. Nosher got the nod but it had been a close shave.

But throughout those years, Nosher was quickly learning more about the trade by sparring with some of the world's greats, like Sugar Ray Robinson, Archie Moore, Jersey Joe Walcott, Muhammad Ali and the great Joe Louis. He also sparred with British talent like Freddie Mills, Bruce Woodcock, Joe Erskine and Joe Bygraves.

Nosher finished his career in the ring defeating a great heavyweight by the name of Menzies Johnson. At the end of that fight, which Nosher won on points, he grabbed the microphone and announced to the Earl's Court crowd, 'I've had a great innings, and I've met some wonderful people. But now I'm hanging up my gloves. God bless you all!'

Nosher had taken the right decision. He had quit the fight game before he lost his marbles or had his brain scrambled taking too much punishment.

Nosher was hardly out of the shower when a man named Jack Isow, who owned Isow's restaurant in Brewer Street, Soho, and the basement club beneath, the Jack of Clubs, walked into his changing room. Isow needed a bouncer he could trust. Nosher wasn't keen until he realised he kept the cloakroom money which amounted to £250 a week. He would be earning around £300 a week working behind bullet-proof glass, in a monkey suit from six 'til three in the morning.

But Nosher would have to earn that money – the hard way. On his very first night trouble tried to walk into the club in the shape of a big, florid, overweight punter. Nosher told him the club was only open to members and the stupid fella took a swing with his right. Nosher grabbed his arm, twisted it behind the man's back and frog-marched him out of the club and into the alley. Nosher knew the boss wouldn't want any members to see how they dealt with trouble.

Once outside, Nosher told him, 'Listen, you fat c—t! Try that again and I'll flatten you.'

The fat bloke threw another right, so Nosher sent him flying into the dustbins and cardboard boxes with a short, crisp right hook. He never set eyes on the fella again.

During the first month, Nosher had to resort to bare-knuckle work almost every other night when objectionable punters tried to throw their weight around. He won every fight. Most fights ended with the uninvited guests rolling among the dustbins or ending spark out on their backs. On other occasions, Nosher had to get really tough, knocking seven shades out of the tough guys who often left behind their teeth, their fillings and a lot of their blood on the ground.

But some guys still tried it on. One smart bastard began by calling out to Nosher, 'Oi, wanker!'

Nosher took up the story. 'I took exception to that, but took a deep breath. "You're having a joke, aren't you, chum?"

' "I don't give a fuck," the geezer replied, "just try throwing me out of this place."

' "Just go downstairs and have a drink with your mate, will you?"

'With that he slams me with a left to the jaw. I shake my head in surprise and disbelief and the whole place went deathly quiet.

'The big lug chimes in, "Go on, chin me."

'I give the customer a gentle tap on the chin.

' "Go on, chin me again," says the geezer, so I give him another light tap.

' "No,' he says, "I'll show you how to punch," and with that he slings a right cross that would have taken off my head if it had landed. Thank goodness the old reflexes were still there and I moved inside the punch, swung him round with my shoulder and planted a haymaker of a right uppercut hitting him full-square on the chin. All 18

NICHOLAS DAVIES / **110**

stone of him went down with a strangulated cry and he's sprawled spark out on the floor.'

When two waiters had carried out the geezer and planted him in a taxi, Nosher walked back into the club and, as one, the whole restaurant stood up and applauded. His Fist of Numbness had done its work once more.

Most of the time, Nosher kept the peace with ease but, of course, on occasions, *real* trouble walked into the club. One night, five likely lads, loud-mouths from the East End, demanded entry and, of course, Nosher told them to leave. They didn't like that.

'Hey, arsehole,' said their yobbish leader, an olive-skinned lad who could have been Maltese. Nosher knew there were a number of small vicious gangs from Greece, Malta and Cyprus dotted around London, always trying to prove something and usually carrying tools like knives, razors and meat cleavers.

Nosher simply said, 'There's the door. Out!'

They left, but Nosher had come across such nasty vicious gangs before and he feared they might wait for him to leave the safety of the club, and then try to take him out. Just in case, Nosher left the club that night with a two-pronged fork up his sleeve.

Nosher left the club and took a long route from the club to the garage where his car was parked. The wet streets of Soho were deserted that night except for two cars parked close together, both containing five men. He was convinced they were waiting for him.

As he drove out of the garage, the two cars followed and, as Nosher drove down to Trafalgar Square, they tailed him. He thought of stopping at New Scotland Yard but realised that, if he did that, the two cars would just drive on. He drove on, cruising slowly through the empty streets, planning what he could do on his own against ten men, tooled up and wanting to knock fuck out of him.

Suddenly he heard a voice behind him. 'Go steady, Nosh!'

He knew that voice and his heart stopped pounding. It was his brother Dinny whom he had phoned earlier and left a message asking him to come urgently to the club as trouble was expected. Dinny hadn't let him down.

Nosher turned left over Chelsea Bridge and then put his foot down hard, accelerating away from the two cars. Across the river, the roads were deserted and the two cars began closing the gap once again.

'Stop now,' yelled Dinny and Nosher slammed on the brakes, swinging the car round in the middle of the road. Dinny threw open the rear door and stood in the middle of the road as the two cars, now abreast, came racing towards him. But Dinny was holding a Beretta shotgun and he was pointing it at the approaching vehicles.

When the cars were only 20 yards away and braking hard, Dinny opened fire, twice. After the second shot, he broke open the gun, slammed in two more cartridges, snapped it back again and fired two more shots.

Both windscreens were shattered and the drivers braked, swung their cars round and raced through the gates of Battersea Park and into a pile of sand bins. Within seconds, the yobs were out of their cars pleading with Dinny to stop firing.

Dinny walked towards them pointing the shotgun at them and all of them raised their hands in surrender.

'I know who you are,' he said. 'You ever come looking

for my brother again and I'll come after you. And next time, it won't be your windscreens – I'll go for your fucking pricks!'

'All right, all right,' they said, got back in their cars and drove away. Nosher never set eyes on them again. But he knew it had been a close shave.

After five years on the door at Isow's, Nosher moved to the Peacock Club in Streatham, South London, where the DJ was a fella who went under the name 'Guy Fawkes'. Unfortunately Guy had fallen foul of a mob from North London and, one Saturday night, a group – ten-handed – turned up.

Nosher saw Guy in the middle of this rough bunch of fellas looking pale and frightened. They were pushing him around and Nosher sensed trouble ahead.

'Leave it out,' he said, 'leave it out.'

Their leader, a weaselly guy, told Nosher to fuck off, but he stood his ground and replied, 'Piss off.'

In a bid to rescue Guy Fawkes, Nosher stepped into the group and grabbed him. The next moment, he felt a thump on his back and a sharp, searing pain wracked his body. One of the bastards had stuck a knife between Nosher's shoulder blades.

But Nosher still had the strength to pull Guy inside the club and slammed the door, jamming the heavy bar down to stop anyone busting in.

Nosher took up the story. 'I felt warm, sticky liquid running down my back, and I knew something bad had happened. In fact, I was bleeding like a stuck pig, and I started to stagger a little. Through the glass door, I saw the mob running away, scattering in different directions. They were gone before the Law arrived.

'I slumped down on a chair waiting for an ambulance. I was fading in and out of consciousness and I could hear the jangling of a bell but I couldn't figure out what was happening. Then I found myself lying face down on a hospital trolley and realised I had only been minutes away from death.

'My back was one mass of red, soaking through my shirt and jacket.

'After examining me, the doctor said, "Mr Powell, you're a very lucky man. You've got such strong back muscles that the blade has glanced off instead of penetrating a vital part. Otherwise, I'd be writing you a death certificate." '

Two days later, Nosher was back working at the club and demanding to know where Weasel Face hung out. He phoned three mates, all three hard nuts, stunt men who could take care of themselves. Nosher asked them along because he had no idea how many foot soldiers the Weasel had at his beck and call.

They walked into the Weasel's club near Oxford Street just as it opened. The room, small and intimate, with discreet lighting, was deserted. On stage was Weasel Face fiddling with the record console.

Nosher walked over to him and, as he looked up, smashed him in the face with a hard right. Nosher slung the records all over the floor, kicked his chair to pieces and up-ended the console. Nosher then pulled the cocktail bar on top of the Weasel as he lay sprawled on the floor. Nosher then grabbed the mic extension lead and wrapped it round the Weasel's neck.

'Listen, c—t,' Nosher said, 'I don't know you from shit and I don't want to. But if you ever try and stick a knife in me again, just make sure you finish the job. I don't use tools, I use hands. And I'll fucking kill you.'

And, as a farewell, Nosher gave him one more almighty whack across the face which knocked him out. Neither Nosher nor his DJ Guy Fawkes ever heard another whisper from their foes in North London.

Nosher went in with his bare knuckles to regain respect throughout London. If Chinese whispers around Soho had reported that Nosher had been fucked over, his credibility would have sunk to zero. Now, word got around that Nosher had taken on a small army of eight bastards and sorted them by himself, beaten the shit out of them. Respect restored.

Nosher was offered jobs working as personal bodyguard to some of the great showbiz stars like Frank Sinatra, Laurence Harvey, Sammy Davis Jr, and others. He was also asked to become the personal minder to one of the world's richest men, the oil mogul Paul Getty. He worked with John Wayne, Bob Hope and Bing Crosby, Robert Morley, Joan Collins and Dorothy Lamour.

And, on occasions, Nosher would find himself having to resort to his bare knuckles when trouble broke out. Even on a film set.

Nosher was employed as a stunt man on the James Bond movie *You Only Live Twice* working alongside Sean Connery.

On this occasion, the stunt co-ordinator, the great Bob Simmons, a veteran of action movies, asked Nosher to run down into a volcano where the launch pad of a rocket was housed. He was to stop at the bottom of a staircase and wait for three explosions. On the third he was told to run across as if heading for the rocket – to put it out of action. As he was running off the set, a fourth explosion would end the scene.

Nosher took up the story of what happened. 'As I heard the director shout "ACTION", I heard the three tremendous explosions and then ran towards the rocket as instructed. As I ran, the fourth explosion hit me full in the face. I had run straight into the blast. I had been told it would go off behind me.

'I was thrown some 20 feet into the air and landed on the hard concrete. I thought I had broken every bone in my body. My head was ringing and I had been winded. I lay on the floor wondering what the hell had gone wrong.

'Dimly, I heard shouts of "CUT, CUT, CUT." People were screaming and yelling. People ran over to me. There was panic.

'Then, through the smoke, Bob Simmons came running saying, "Fantastic, fucking fantastic," and grinning from ear to ear.

'I asked Bob why the last explosion had hit me in the face.

'He replied, "If I'd told you that, you wouldn't have run into it."

'I then realised the bastard had set me up, so that he got a great action shot for his fucking movie. I was very, very angry.'

Three days later, Nosher returned to the set bruised and battered and still half-deaf, taking his brother Dinny with him as back-up.

The two men approached Bob Simmons while he was chatting to another extra. They just stood and stared at him as he turned more pale by the minute.

'Why hello, Nosher,' said Simmons, being friendly.

With those words, Dinny hit him with a massive haymaker and Simmons sank to the floor like a fucking felled tree. There was blood all over Simmon's shirt but it was Dinny's blood. He had hit the bastard so hard he had split open his knuckles!

Some thirty stunt men who were standing around looked on with their mouths open. On a word from Nosher, they carried him off the set and into the stunt room. Simmons came round and tried to get to his feet. Nosher told him to lie still.

'Piss off,' said Simmons.

That was the signal Nosher wanted. Now it was his turn to let Simmons know what it was like to have a bomb explode in your face. Nosher hit him with all the force in his body, the knuckles of his right fist smashing Simmons on the jaw. He collapsed, spark out. Nosher went off looking for Dinny and they went to the canteen for a coffee.

Some while later, Simmons walked in, rubbing his jaw and Nosher went over to him. 'Listen,' he said, 'you nearly got me killed. I could have accepted that – but I can't accept the way you did it. If you had warned me about what you really planned, we could have discussed it. But you never said nothing. Now, don't ever do that to me again.' And Nosher walked out.

CHAPTER 7

Charlie Bronson is a man no one messes with, ever! He is not proud of the reputation; it's simply a fact of life. 'If you're going to come at me,' Bronson warns everyone, 'you must be prepared to knock me unconscious or kill me. I fear no one. Violence just makes me madder and stronger.'

Charles Bronson has spent 23 of the last 27 years in solitary confinement in top-security jails across Britain. He is the most feared convict in the entire prison system. He has been locked in dungeons, in iron boxes concreted in the middle of cells and, famously, in a cage like the fictional anti-hero Hannibal Lecter.

He has endured more periods of isolation than any other living British prisoner, spending months at a time with nothing more than cockroaches for company. He is always held in maximum security in a spartan cell with only a concrete bed with a fire-proof mattress and a table and chair made from compressed cardboard. Whenever he is allowed out for his daily one-hour exercise stint – or moved to another jail – 12 police officers in riot gear and with dogs escort him.

But during a brief taste of freedom Charlie Bronson entered Britain's secret world of bare-knuckle fighting and won instant acclaim for his violence and ferocity. Those who thrill to the spectacle of a really violent man going hammer and tongs in a bare-knuckle fight all recall the day they saw Charlie Bronson in action. It was a sight never to be forgotten and is still talked about today in the pubs and clubs where such contests are held in high esteem.

People begin to understand Bronson when they hear the names that have been used to describe him – Mad Man, Danger Man, Violent Man, One-man Army, Disruptive and Disturbed Man! He has been on a mission of madness, a mission of destruction, within the entire prison system. Throughout his life, Charlie has been officially observed, monitored, analysed and assessed by the authorities on countless occasions.

But Charlie sees it quite differently. He wrote in his autobiography:

> *In jail they watch me every day, all day. They watch me like a buzzard watches its prey and a mongoose watches a cobra. I'm trapped, caught up in a web, like a fly that's been captured by a spider.*
>
> *A few of us end up in a cage like some*

birds, lions or elephants end up caged. Prison is a human zoo, a cage of man.

After 27 years of looking through the bars and searching my own mind, I am now convinced it's all been my test in life. I have been through an incredible journey at the very heart of Britain's penal system. My journey included countless beatings; drug control; isolation; asylums; roof-top protests; hostages; violence and hunger-strikes.

Fate has been cruel to me but I'm still fighting; and I'll probably die fighting the system. I acknowledge that I have been described as Britain's most violent prisoner. And to get a label like that doesn't come overnight. It takes years of agony and pain and oceans of emptiness.

For every punch I've thrown in prison I have taken a dozen in return. The penal system caters for everyone. Where one screw is needed for one prisoner, six will look after another – and the ringing of the alarm bell will bring 60 more. I've been throwing punches from the day I entered prison.

I've lost count of the number of screws I've punched and they've probably lost count of the times they've punched me. But throughout these years, I've learnt to my cost that there is only one loser – myself. I know now that I may as well have punched a door or nut a wall. I know the best way to rid yourself of aggression is in the gym, for every

*punch I've thrown has lost me a little bit
more of my life.*

*To keep my sanity, I still train in my cell
day and night as I have done for the past 20
years. For as long as I can remember, I've
been king of the press-ups and sit-ups. I am
on record as having completed 1,727 press-
ups in one hour! I am also on record as
having completed 25 press-ups with two men
lying on my back.*

Charles Bronson, whose real name is Michael Gordon
Peterson, took his name from the American film actor
who spent much of his career playing tough guys. Born
in Luton, Bedfordshire, in 1952, he had enjoyed a
happy, disciplined, loving family life with his parents
and his two brothers but he always yearned for
excitement. He married his childhood sweetheart Irene
and they had a son Michael who was three when
Charlie's life changed for ever.

One day in 1974, at the age of 21, Charlie broke
out; he went wild. Charlie indulged in one week of
sheer, complete, unadulterated madness. And the only
reason he knows why he behaved like that – which at
the time was totally out of character – was because he
suddenly and dramatically craved excitement.

One day, his violent urges simply overcame him. He
got himself a shotgun, sawed down the barrel and went
to work as an armed robber. In one week of insanity he
robbed a post office, a garage and a Tudor mansion.
During that week of violence and mayhem, he even
stuck the shotgun up a bloke's arse and was only a

fraction away from pulling the trigger and committing murder.

Extraordinarily, Bronson never tried to blame anything or anyone for that week of madness. He admitted to himself and the authorities that he had nothing or no one to blame but himself. He wasn't on drugs and he hardly ever drank alcohol. The only way he has ever been able to explain his week of insanity was the buzz, the excitement, the exhilaration he yearned for and his brain demanded. He accepted that, when he was captured, the courts would have no option but to remand him in custody.

After pleading guilty, he was jailed for seven years. With remission for good behaviour, he would only have to serve four years and eight months. But both seemed an eternity to such a wild young man.

Six months into his sentence, Charlie was permitted his first visit from Irene and Michael. They were permitted just one hour together. When they walked away, Charlie could sense they were slipping away from him and the thought of losing them for ever would wind him up until he was ready to tear himself apart.

Instead, in his desperation, he broke a con's nose and smashed up his ribs with his bare fists. He took out his frustration on the convict and felt better; he had emptied himself of a terrible rage. A few days later, he smashed up a grass because Charlie felt hatred bubbling up inside him.

Charlie confessed later, 'It was as if I was on a suicide mission. I hit him with hooks and crosses. Insanely, I even tried to gouge his eye out. I was so far gone I was actually enjoying it.'

More rationally, he went on, 'I understood that violence is an escape from reality; helping to relieve tension. In prison, the law of the jungle prevails. The victor will earn respect. It's truly mad but that's the reality of prison life. I left the filthy grass on the lavatory floor in his own blood and dirt. I walked out on my own to be escorted to the punishment block.'

Some of Charlie's violent actions resulted in yet more months being added to his four years and eight months inside. And he didn't like that.

Charlie didn't like being told what to do by the screws whom he didn't respect. Charlie took an instant dislike to one screw, a big bloke and a former rugby player, who always tried to order him around. One day, the rugby player went too far and upset Charlie.

Charlie had been kicked out of the workshop where he was being trained to use a sewing machine because he kept sabotaging the equipment. Instead, he spent his days playing scrabble and poker, chatting to mates and drinking tea. Charlie liked that. Then the screw started his bollocks.

Charlie said later, 'So I smashed the shop to bits – the furniture, the windows, the lights, the office. I told the other cons to stay clear and then I picked up a broken table and threw it at the advancing screws, hitting one on the crust. The alarm bells sounded as they carried him out of the shop.

'I could hear the screws running towards the workshop, then there was silence. One screw strolled into the room as if it was a picnic and tells me quietly, "Put that stick down before I ram it up your arse."

'I did as I was told. I put it down ... sixty miles an hour over his crust! I went to smash him again but they were on me like a ton of bricks and I was pinned down. They carried me out. I couldn't breathe. I was choking and some bastard was squeezing my balls as hard as he could. Fists were smashing into my body. By the time they got me to the punishment block, I was well and truly fucked. Pain is not the word. My bollocks were in agony, my body ached, my eye was cut and even my toes were throbbing with pain.

'They stripped me naked and strapped me into a body-belt. This is a leather belt that locks at the back and has a metal cuff on each hip, which locks the wrists. They also strapped my ankles. Then they injected my right buttock with a hypodermic needle.

'I realised they had injected me with the infamous "liquid cosh", the strong sedative which has since been banned. The drug, a large dose of Largactil, knocked me out and when I awoke there was blood and vomit all around me. The side-effects were even worse; stiffness, muscular spasms, dry mouth and blurry vision which lingered for days.

'I woke up in the "strong-box", a double-doored cell, sound-proofed and totally isolated. It's like a cell within a cell with no windows and no furniture. It's deathly silent.'

For that outburst of violence, Charlie was given an extra six months' sentence.

A few months later, Charlie received yet another six-month addition to his sentence, once again for assaulting the guards. It seemed he was losing his mind, losing control, and he seemed unable to stem his violent outbursts which were becoming more prevalent. Sometimes, Charlie turned his violence towards other cons.

One night, a Scot named John Henry Gallagher, who inhabited the cell above him, kept banging on the floor and, no matter how many times Charlie called on him to stop, he refused. Charlie was getting angry, very angry, and he was determined to teach the Scotsman a lesson. For two days, his frustration and anger simmered until he saw a chance for revenge.

Charlie remembers what happened. 'I tore into his cell with a jug and smashed it into his face. I hit him again and again with the jagged handle. He screamed for help so I kept hitting him. Each whack was with the jug handle and it cut him every time – legs, body, arms, face, chest and neck. I just kept cutting the bastard and he just kept screaming. Towards the end, I was laughing every time I cut him and I suddenly realised I was laughing insanely.'

But Charlie knew full well what was happening to him. He knew the danger signs when he realised he no longer felt any emotions except for one – hate.

He believed prison had made him a madman. The screws came and grabbed Charlie and took him off to the punishment block, his own clothes almost dripping blood from the wounded Scot. He now faced a GBH charge.

But the prison authorities then decided that Charlie had to be kept away from other cons, destined to live a life of solitary confinement because he was considered too dangerous to permit him to mix with the general prison population. So he began a life of to'ing and fro'ing, being moved every few months from one maximum security jail to another.

Charlie planned a routine to survive his life of isolation, boredom and total loneliness. He began to get fit, to train in an effort to survive the 23 hours a day he would spend in solitary confinement. Press-ups, sit-ups, squats, step-ups and shadow boxing. During his one hour in the exercise yard, he jogged. He did this every day except Sunday.

But Charlie's violence would keep erupting at the most innocuous incidents. A screw who upset him or insulted him would be butted or battered; another convict would be smashed up for just looking at Charlie or making a remark. He was continually moved from one maximum security prison to another and most of the time he was immediately sent to the punishment block and the one thing he hated above all else – solitary confinement.

Understandably, the isolation finally got to him. He would hear voices or noises when there was no one outside his cell and, if he saw people talking, he believed they were always talking about him. He even attacked the doctor who came to examine him but was restrained before he did any damage. He knew he was rapidly becoming insane and the news that his beloved wife Irene wanted to divorce him made his life seem utterly useless.

Charlie felt that his entire life had become a daily battle against the screws and the system. He felt everyone treated him with contempt and he believed that hate and bitterness was eating away his insides. He felt intense bitterness towards nearly everyone and that affected his health, his diet, his sleep, his bowels and his mind. He was stressed out and anxious. Indeed, he got to such a stage that he hated himself for being so hateful. Then, to cap all his fears, Charlie became totally and hopelessly clinically depressed.

He now cared for nothing. He felt empty. His life had spun out of control and he felt a hollowness inside his mind and his body. He was a superbly fit young man but his brain was in turmoil. Four years in Britain's jails had transformed him from a healthy, fit, young go-getter into a sick old man.

Indeed, Charlie felt no pain and no anguish when he took a razor and sliced through his own wrists and arms. As he cut himself up, he felt no love in his heart, not even for himself. But that, however, was only a prelude to the actions he took some weeks later when he really fucked up.

One Sunday, Charlie was up early and keen for the hours to pass because his beloved cousin Loraine was coming to visit him. For the first time for months, he felt fresh and alive and, more importantly, totally sane. Then one of the screws annoyed him.

Once again, Charlie lost his cool and, when the warder gave him his breakfast, Charlie went for him, cutting him across the face. All hell broke loose but this time Charlie was ready for a real fight. He and the warder were half-killing each other before a dozen other officers arrived. Finally, they dragged the warder and Charlie apart. Charlie was taken to the punishment block, the warder to hospital.

They left Charlie in a punishment cell naked, beaten, aching and utterly demoralised. He sank to the depths of despair, realising his life had become a senseless existence, violent and loveless. And he began crying, not for himself, but for Loraine, Ian and Pam who were travelling that day to Parkhurst on the Isle of Wight to visit him for the first time for months. Of course, they were not permitted to see him and had to return home.

Charlie was given some powerful drugs to calm him down and he was taken to court. The judge sectioned him under the Mental Health Act and he was sent to Rampton Secure Hospital in Nottinghamshire for an indefinite stay. Though drugged, Charlie realised this meant he was being sentenced to life with no release date.

It was only a matter of months before Charlie earned the title of Rampton's Public Enemy Number One mainly because he all but strangled a paedophile to death with a neck-tie. Charlie asked for the police to be called so they would issue a charge of attempted murder against him, but the authorities refused, saying he was 'too disturbed' to stand trial.

So they sent him to Broadmoor instead.

He found the place horrific. Charlie described it as a monster's paradise and a psychiatrist's dream. He was to stay there for five very long years and, for most of that time, he was forced to take very powerful anti-psychotic drugs. Charlie ballooned from a superbly fit and healthy 12 stone to over 17 stone; he became fat, weak, breathless and exhausted.

Helped by a couple of mates, including Ronnie Kray, Charlie began his training routine once again. It was tough, going through hell every day, to return to fitness and better health. Then Charlie had the idea of escaping from Broadmoor and this excited him, driving him to peak physical condition so he would be superbly fit when the moment of escape arrived.

Indeed, Charlie became the first lunatic to break free and get on to a roof in Broadmoor in over 100 years. Later, Charlie recalled his bid to escape,

'The rain was chucking it down that day but I had made my decision. Twelve of us were being escorted to the canteen when I made my dash for freedom. I ran towards a slippery beam and climbed on it, but only after kicking a screw in the face who tried to stop me. I dived through a cell window and made my way up a drainpipe. Up I went! I was on top of Broadmoor and on top of the world! The rain was pouring down in sheets but it felt magic. I was free.

'Then I began my mission of destruction. Slates flew through cell and office windows in the building opposite. I aimed the slates at workshop windows and anybody within distance. I tore out electrical wires, TV aerials, copper pipes and timber. They had to evacuate the ward beneath me and turn off the water supply and electricity. For hours, I went on the rampage, emptying myself of the years of pain and mental anguish I had somehow survived. The hatred seemed to ooze out of me. Every slate I slung off that roof represented a day of my life caged up. I started laughing, shouting, singing and screaming. Madness enveloped me. My hands were bleeding and my head was cut and my body was soaked with the rain, sweat, blood, grime and dirt. My eyes were full of dust, my muscles ached and my back was sore – but I loved every minute of it.

'My mission of destruction finally came to an end near nightfall. I was completely shattered and exhausted. I found a place out of the way of the searchlights and lay down. This was the first night I'd spent looking up at the stars for eight years. Eight fucked-up years.'

The following day, Charlie came down of his own volition because he knew that on this occasion he could not make good his escape. He decided to leave the roof, take the shit they would hand out and start to get fit again for one further attempt to escape.

Whenever depression set in, Charlie fought it in his own unique way. He plotted his next escape bid. The authorities had to watch him each and every day. They could sense that he was planning some adventure because he was training throughout the day, getting fitter and stronger by the minute. His mood also changed from black depression and hopelessness to a sort of cheerful self-confidence.

When he made his next attempt some months later, he was once again able to climb on to the roof and become King of the Castle once more. Somehow, Charlie managed to climb 60 feet to the roof up a 100-year-old drainpipe that was falling apart. This time, however, he had the run of two roofs and he totally demolished both of them. It was a glorious hot, summer's day and Charlie was in his element, singing, laughing and tearing the place apart. He named himself The Governor of Broadmoor and called that day, 'the happiest day of my life'.

For three days, Charlie destroyed the roofs of two of the wards. He threw slates at parked cars and at windows and tore out the water pipes and the electricity cables. Television crews and photographers turned out to film him and he was headline news on the nightly programmes. He also made the national newspapers under the headline, KILLER ON THE ROOF.

Charlie discovered heaven while destroying the roofs, removing both the slates and the huge wooden rafters. He would describe the nights on the roof as 'being in paradise'.

In the end, the only reason Charlie gave up his roof-top protest was because of his mother. Both his father and his brother Mark came to talk to him, to persuade him to come down because of the anxiety his protest was causing his mother. He came down because he knew that, throughout his life he had caused her so much heartache and stress. He didn't want her health to be ruined by his actions. He was also bloody hungry!

It was after this protest that Charlie started to write and to draw. He began by writing poetry and became known as the 'Psychopathic Poet'. He also began drawing cartoons. He found it calmed his nerves, gave him something to occupy his mind, and filled his day during the endless hours of solitary confinement. Indeed, such was Charlie's enthusiasm, he quickly became the convict who won more prison awards than anyone else for his poems, prose and cartoons. It made him feel good, too.

Charlie was sent back to Walton Jail and that made him feel like making another escape bid. He had discovered at Broadmoor that the inmates – the loonies as he called them – only jeered and took the piss when he made his escapes. He anticipated that the cons in

Walton would cheer and feed him if he ever made a roof-top protest.

So he decided to give it a go. He had felt so exhilarated, so relaxed and so wonderful throughout his last protest, he simply wanted to enjoy life once again and he knew no better way than to shin up a drainpipe on to a roof and destroy the fucking jail!

So he did. Despite another near-impossible climb up rickety drainpipes and guttering, Charlie again made it to the roof. Only this time, the cons were totally on his side, cheering him on and singing, 'There's only one Micky Peterson, only one Micky Peterson ...'

For the next three days, Charlie demolished the place – slates, timber, windows, skylights – on four wings. The Scousers cheered him on and passed him food, drink and blankets. Some even got nicked for helping him. The prison authorities sent up a hit team to try to grab Charlie and bring him down.

As they walked along the roof towards him, Charlie warned them, 'Come near me and I'll jump and take one of you with me. I'll grab the first one of you and jump off.' The crazy thing was that Charlie meant it, and they knew it, too. They didn't take him on.

Once again, Charlie agreed to come down on the promise that a date for a tribunal to study Charlie's application for freedom would be made. The authorities agreed, Charlie's lawyer came to ensure fair play and Charlie came down facing a bill for £100,000 of damage!

At the four-hour tribunal, presided over by a High Court judge, Charlie argued that he wasn't a psychopath or a schizophrenic. They couldn't even agree why he was ever in a hospital for the criminally insane. Charlie knew the score. He knew he had been certified mad because of his violent ways. He was still violent, but now they were certifying him as sane! The Judge gave Charlie an absolute discharge but he first had to complete a four-year sentence. Then, at last, he would be a free man.

That day did finally arrive and Charlie was out of the prison gates at 100 miles an hour. Nothing could stop him now. He was a free man.

After spending some time with his parents in Wales, Charlie was heading back to London intent on sticking to the advice given him by Reggie Kray. 'You could be a great prize-fighter,' Reggie had told him 100 times while they were in prison together. 'You have so much aggression inside you and you're really fit and strong. When you get out of this shit-hole, go for it, get into the fight game, the *real* fight game, bare-knuckle stuff. If you don't do something to earn good money, you'll just end up back inside. Go out and win.'

So Charlie went to gymnasiums in and around London, sparring with proper boxers, learning the tricks of the trade. He also did weights, swam and did some running. At last, Charlie was living a real life and he got rid of all his madness and aggression by working out and getting fit. Within a matter of weeks, Charlie was fit and strong and ready for his first bare-knuckle fight.

In his autobiography, Charlie re-lived that first fight.

'It was to be held above a pub – obviously I can't say where, because it was illegal. I won. It was so easy, it was untrue! I hit him with 14 years of hell inside me. I got paid £500, a lot of money when you've got fuck-all.'

After that victory, Charlie knew that he could make a fucking good living from prize-fighting. He was only 35 years old, 14 stone, solid, fast, fit and full of aggression. He didn't smoke or drink or take drugs and he had 14 years of madness inside him that he needed to release, frequently.

It was at this time that Charlie decided to change his name – officially – to Charles Bronson, after the American film actor of that name. Interestingly, Charlie had never seen a Charles Bronson film neither was he attracted to the tough-guy persona. In fact, his gaffer – Paul Edmonds – chose the name, and it stuck.

The room above the secret East End pub was always holding bare-knuckle fights and the place was full of ex-cons placing a few bets. Charlie liked the atmosphere, but not as much as the money he wanted to make from winning bare-knuckle contests.

His next opponent was the famous 'Bermondsey Bear', an awesome man with loads of black body hair, a shaven skull, toothless and covered in tattoos. As soon as Charlie saw him – growling, swearing and eye-balling him, Charlie knew he could take him, for the Bermondsey Bear was also slow and unfit.

Charlie recalled that fight, saying, 'I knew I had to hurt him badly. As I looked at him, I pictured every stinking screw that ever stuck the boot in my head, every bad prison doctor, every slag governor and I fucking hated him.'

To the men in his corner, Charlie growled, 'I gonna kill this fat c—t. But first I'm going to make him scream.'

Charlie wrote in his book,

> *The crowd wanted a good fight, and they got it. Ding! Ding! I ran out of my corner and smashed a right into the middle of his ugly face. He slung a few punches but they all missed. I caught him a peach in the ribs and heard him wince. Then he kneed me in the bollocks and pain shot through me like a red-hot poker. I felt sick, dizzy. Then he nutted me and dug a thumb in my eye. But the bell saved me.*
>
> *As I sat in my corner recovering, I vowed that the bastard had done all the damage he would ever do to me.*
>
> *In the second round I quickly nutted him, splitting his nose open. Then I really opened up on him – 20 or 30 shots to the head. Ten would have done. As he fell over, I fell on top of him. Now I had lost it. Now it was my turn to do the damage. I put my whole weight on his windpipe and he couldn't breathe. Then guys jumped into the ring pulling me off him, hitting me, trying to get me off his windpipe. Luckily for him, they did.*

Charlie had won and he earned himself another handsome purse. He was enjoying life.

But Charlie's next fight earned him nothing. The money he earned in that prize-fight all went to a young leukaemia victim. There were six fights in the pub and

Charlie easily won. The kid died later but the money raised that night was enough to send him on a dream holiday to Disneyworld in Florida.

Charlie Bronson challenged the great Lenny McLean to a bare-knuckle fight, but Lenny had retired from the fight game and didn't want to know. Charlie even offered to put up £5,000 of his own money but Lenny couldn't be persuaded. But there were others who realised that Charlie was becoming a very powerful figure in the unlicensed, ferocious world of bare-knuckle fighting. Some gave him the title of 'The Uncrowned Champion'.

Charlie's third fight was against a gypsy champion named Romany Ron but the fight didn't even last one round. The fight with Ron netted £800 for him, but Charlie was after the big fish in fights which would earn him £5,000! Charlie needed to fight to keep his madness and his aggression under control but the fighters prepared to box him bare-knuckle were few and far between. So, friends suggested he take on a Rottweiler, a real, huge beast of a dog that had won a string of fights against other fighters.

Charlie wrote, 'The place was packed that night and the fans were screaming. I looked at that huge, snarling hulk of a ferocious animal and feared he might actually win. I knew I had to strike first before he could floor me and tear me to pieces. I managed to punch it in the mouth and as my hand was in its jaws – as it was about to rip my arm off – I just kept smashing my fist as far down its throat as possible. As it was going down there was froth coming out of its mouth. It was a terrible sight. But I knocked it right down and in one mighty swoop I ripped out half its lungs. I had killed it. Not a nice thing to do, but when you're getting paid ten grand it's a lot of money when you've got nothing.'

But all Charlie's determination to go straight and keep out of trouble eventually came to a crashing finale and all because he wanted to give his darling 18-year-old girlfriend – a beautiful young woman by the name of Alison – something special for Christmas. He wanted to give her a ring. But, being Charlie Bronson, he thought he might as well take some other things from the Luton jeweller's, not just one ring.

He explained what happened as he went to get his beloved Alison a lovely Christmas present. 'I ran into the jeweller's shop and there were three people in the shop, two men and a woman. I made them all lie on the floor, pointed the gun at them and filled the bag. I grabbed the cash, too, and shot off. Tally-ho! Happy Christmas. It was a piece of cake. I parcelled it all up, except for one ring, and delivered the parcel to a fence. The job was done. I went to see Alison and put the beautiful ring on her finger.'

Two weeks later – on his sixty-ninth day of freedom – Charlie was out jogging as usual when he went to run past a well-built labourer walking towards him. *Smack!* The labourer cracked him a fierce blow on the jaw. The next moment Charlie was in a strangle-hold and the labourer was saying, 'You're under arrest, Bronson, for suspicion of armed robbery.'

Somehow, the cops had known that Charlie had committed the robbery but for the first time in his life they were calling him 'Charlie Bronson', and not by his former name. Despite a lack of evidence and no witnesses, Charlie found himself back in court and all because his innocent young Alison had told the police about the ring. Charlie got seven years. He was back inside once more.

But jail got to Charlie again and, after being moved to the latest, ultra-modern top-security jail, Long Lartin in Worcestershire, he went berserk.

In his book, Charlie wrote:

> *Late one night, I got out of bed and covered myself in black boot polish from head to toe. I was now bollock starkers and black as soot. I then smashed a glass bottle over my head. The blood trickled down my face and neck. Fuck knows to this day why I did it.*
>
> *Next, I secured the broken bottle on to a broom handle like a spear. Then I tied one red rag around my forehead and another round my right bicep, lay on my bed and waited for morning to arrive. I felt strange. My head was throbbing and there was blood and black polish all over me and my bed. Long Lartin has electric doors, and as soon as I heard the click, I walked out straight towards the screws.*
>
> *One spotted me soon enough and his face turned white. He ran to sound the alarm bell and I ran into the association room. I picked up the TV and slung it at the bars. It exploded. Then I tore out the lights and smashed about 40 chairs before tearing the door off its hinges. I also smashed out the*

*giant plate-glass windows. Some of the glass
cut my feet and other parts of my body but I
didn't care. I felt great!*

*I ran into the next TV room and smashed
up that one as well and I could hear lots of
commotion outside and the cons all
screaming and yelling, adding to the
confusion. Nothing lasts for ever and the
heavy mob came in and I was put in the
strong-box and given an injection. I slept for
days.*

Moved from one top-security jail to another all over
Britain, Charlie had some quiet times, but he
continually found himself under intense pressure,
needing some action in his life, needing to get rid of his
aggression. One day, while in Frankland, Durham's top-
security jail, Charlie saw a stranger while exercising in
the yard with 200 other cons. For no apparent reason,
Charlie saw the man – wearing a suit and tie and
sporting a beard – as a target.

Charlie closed in on the stranger, grabbed him,
slung him over his shoulder and legged it into an office.
The cons were cheering but the warders were worried
shitless. The stranger Charlie had taken hostage was
the prison's deputy governor! But Charlie saw reason
when he was told his hostage was the deputy governor
and, after informal chats with mates, he let him walk
out.

In November 1992, Charlie Bronson was a free man
once again. His family found him a little flat in New
Brighton on Merseyside and he even found a job as a

doorman for a nightclub working just two nights a week. Charlie was relaxed and happy, working out in the gym every day, eating well, and breathing fresh, clean air and free!

But he busted open a man's nose, a fella he found in an old girlfriend's flat, and a mob of cops arrested him after a tussle. Within hours, they also charged him with conspiracy to rob a bank, possession of a firearm and grievous bodily harm.

After just 55 days of freedom, Charlie was back in jail once again, though this time he claimed to be totally innocent. But, understandably, jail got to him and he was now an angry and bitter man. He tried to take a screw hostage but, fortunately for him, the screw escaped. Two of the charges were dropped and Charlie was taken to court to face the GBH charge over the man's broken nose. He was fined £600 and freed!

But 16 days later, Charlie's world fell apart once again. He was sitting in a mate's car happily chatting away, when out of nowhere armed cops surrounded the vehicle. There were guns pointing at his head from all angles. He was taken to Woodhill Prison in Milton Keynes and was once again charged with conspiracy to rob a bank and possession of a shotgun. Someone was determined to make the charges stick.

It was while he was on remand at Woodhill, waiting for trial that Charlie took his second hostage. He had just finished 600 press-ups and was feeling so strong and keen that, in a moment's rush of blood to the head, he kidnapped a screw named Andy Love whom, ironically, Charlie respected.

Looking back on that incident, Charlie said, 'I was

actually simply craving company, craving humanity. I had really enjoyed and done well when I was out in the real world, meeting real people. Now, here I was banged up again on a debatable charge and I needed companionship.

'I just wanted a chat with someone, a cup of tea with someone, maybe a game of Scrabble. Isolation gets to a man, particularly after 20 years of being locked up. And if the prison authorities refused me real company, I wanted a blow-up doll.'

They didn't like that idea. They argued that if Charlie was allowed a blow-up doll, every convict in the whole jail would demand one. Negotiations went on for 17 hours, with Charlie demanding an axe, a machine-gun, 10,000 rounds of ammunition and a helicopter out of the jail or a blow-up doll. In the end, poor Andy Love farted and Charlie blew his top, telling the guards to get Andy out of the place. Unbelievably, the authorities charged Charlie with 'making an unwarranted demand for an inflatable doll contrary to Section 21 of the Theft Act 1968'!

At his trial on the bank charge, Charlie was only found guilty of possessing a shotgun with intent to rob and not guilty on the more serious conspiracy charge. It seemed to make no difference to the judge; Charlie was given eight years for intent to rob and two years for possession. He was gutted.

Once again, Charlie Bronson was on the move, from one maximum-security jail to another; and, once again, he took hostage another prison governor, Adrian Wallace, of Hull. Once again that siege came to an end and no one was injured. Now, Charlie Bronson had quite a reputation for taking people hostage and the Home Office hadn't a clue how to handle such a convict. They just kept moving him from jail to jail.

Finally, the decision was taken to move Charlie into the most gruesome isolation cage ever built within Britain's entire prison – The Hannibal Cage in Wakefield Prison. This cage, the only one of its kind in the UK, had only been used once to house Bob Maudsley, jailed for life in 1974 for stabbing and garrotting his uncle. While in Wakefield, he killed three convicts, one of whom he decapitated and then ate his brains with a spoon!

Charlie would write in his book,

The cage was a living death, a total void. It had its own toilet and shower so there is no human contact with any other cons. All meals are put on a table ten feet away from the cage doors. When I was unlocked to collect my meal, there were no fewer than a dozen screws standing by. Once I counted fifteen.

This procedure happened three times a day. It was the only time that I actually left my cell. I was not allowed any exercise, neither was I allowed any visits apart from legal ones. When my probation officer or solicitor visited me, they had to sit outside the cage door. The outer door is made of solid steel and has an observation slit in it. The inner door is also steel, with a steel net across it. The inner door had a 12in-wide gap at the bottom through which cups of tea could be passed.

Sheets of bullet-proof glass formed one section of the cell wall. Through these, I could be observed 24 hours a day. My table and chair were made of compressed cardboard and my cutlery and plates were plastic. My bed was bolted to the concrete floor. The walls were reinforced steel and concrete; the bars on the window solid steel. A steel cage is attached to the outside of the window.

This cage was the end of the line. The silence is the madness. Fantasy becomes reality. There is nothing to look at, no one to talk to, no one to listen to you. You feel like the living dead. Dreams and nightmares, day and night, merge seamlessly. You are empty, utterly empty.

After taking several other people hostage, Charlie is now in prison for life and he believes he will never get out alive, unless he escapes. He feels like a fly in a spider's web, trapped, unable to escape. He also has visions of destroying himself one day.

He wrote at the end of his autobiography, 'I know I'm no psychopath because I have a conscience and I do feel guilt. There are two sides to me. If I like a person, I'd die for them. If I hate them, they may die for me. Just pray you never get on my bad side. My bad side is your worst enemy.'

CHAPTER 8

The world of bare-knuckle fighting is secret, forbidding and challenging. Those men in the know keep their secrets close to their chests because they know if they open their 'traps', the police, big trouble and court appearances will follow.

When fighters talk between themselves, their language can sound like gobbledegook because they don't want outsiders to understand precisely what they are saying. They often use false names and code names for many of the places where bare-knuckle fights take place today, because the law believes such sport should be stopped.

Fights take place throughout Britain in car parks, behind pubs and clubs, in motorway petrol stations, lorry parks and sometimes in a field in the middle of the countryside. Some fights take place in pubs, but those who attend are closely scrutinised. No one can take risks, especially the person whose pub or club is the venue. For a fight to take place anywhere, there are some ground rules. The venue must be easily accessible to motorists because those bare-knuckle enthusiasts and the punters who enjoy betting on fights travel to the contests just before proceedings are due to begin. No one in the sport wants to advertise the fact that a fight is about to take place; in fact, the very opposite.

Despite the restrictions, and despite the necessity of keeping bare-knuckle contests secret, most fights between known boxers will be watched by several hundred fellas, whilst a top-of-the-bill bare-knuckle contest between two well-known combatants will draw crowds of several thousand.

When you stand and watch the enthusiasm and the spirit among those attending the fight you realise how exciting and pitiless bare-knuckle fighting really is. The screams and the yells, the hopes and despair, the knock-downs and the great punches are watched by people who understand and appreciate the sport and the art involved. To people who know little or nothing about it, bare-knuckle boxing is classed as violent, outrageous, cruel, brutal and even degrading. But those who love the sport understand the great strength and courage of the fighters, the honour and respect of those taking part. They also understand the remarkable courage, fitness and tenacity of the fighters to take such punishment and still come back for more.

And, despite what the sport's detractors might say, it's not just for money. There are a vast proprtion of onlookers who choose not to place a bet at all. The great majority of the punters thoroughly enjoy a bare-knuckle fight as much as a football fan enjoys and appreciates watching Manchester United versus Arsenal or a cricket enthusiast watching England play Australia for the Ashes. But those who don't understand the sport don't understand the sheer masculinity, aggression and total dedication to becoming a champion which drives those who take part.

Of course, some fighters only become involved as a way to earn their living, pay the rent, feed the kids. Some fellas get involved because they've just come out of prison and can't get a regular job. Today, many recruits to the sport take it up as soon as they leave prison because they emerge into civvy street in peak physical condition and realise that bare-knuckle fighting can earn them much-needed money. So many prisoners nowadays have the time and the facilities in jail to become superbly fit, doing hundreds of press-ups and sit-ups a day, doing weights, skipping, running and even eating healthy food.

Some boxers, who have fought in licensed bouts, turn to bare-knuckle contests if they believe they have little chance of reaching the top. They soon learn they can earn far more money fighting bare-knuckle than they can being seventh or eighth on the bill of a licensed boxing match. Some boxers keep up licensed fighting and dabble in bare-knuckle fights.

And then, of course, most importantly, are the 'pikeys', the Romanies and gypsies who move from place to place throughout the UK. To the gypsies, bare-knuckle fighting is the *only* way to fight. The gypsy teenagers are trained by their fathers and uncles to box and to fight. They spar from a young age; they learn to be quick on their feet and with their fists. And they learn to punch hard, to wrestle, to throw a man; they learn the strangle-holds and the leg-holds. When the going gets tough, they also must know how to defend themselves, to grapple, to kick and, if necessary, to head-butt and to bite.

Bare-knuckle boxing and fighting is part of gypsy folklore and the practice goes on today in the majority of the traditional families. The fighters not only box for the winner's purse and the side-bets but also, more importantly, for the honour of their family. To be a champion bare-knuckle fighter is to be a distinguished member of the gypsy fraternity and with such titles come respect and honour, as well as hard cash.

There are, in reality, only a handful of promoters capable of organising the top-level bouts today. And they have to take extreme care. With the sophisticated surveillance equipment now available to the police, the promoters have to tread very carefully; the law can hand out prison sentences for organising such unlicensed fights where only bare-knuckles are permitted.

One of the few men in Britain who knows most of the top bare-knuckle fighters personally is Billy Cribb, whose forefathers have been involved in the sport for generations. His uncle was a bare-knuckle champion who won the title of The Guv'nor of Barnet Fair over many, many years.

In the world of bare-knuckle boxing, winning the title of The Guv'nor is the equivalent of winning a

oe Pyle: the man who brought Roy Shaw and Lenny McLean together.

Charles Bronson in the ring during one of his rare spells on the outside.

Bronson keeping in shape during his time in Hull Prison.

The young Nosher Powell.

Woe betide the challenger of this man!

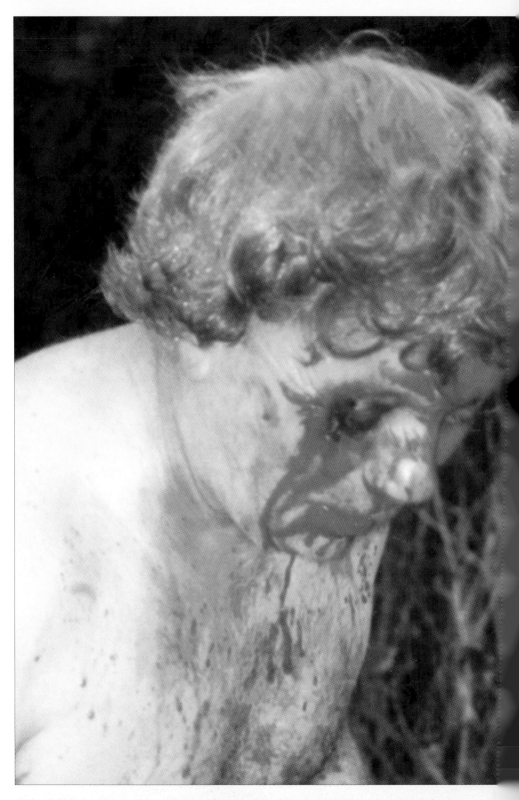

Billy Cribb, bare-knuckle veteran, bloodied and bruised. Billy's own book is due out in 2001

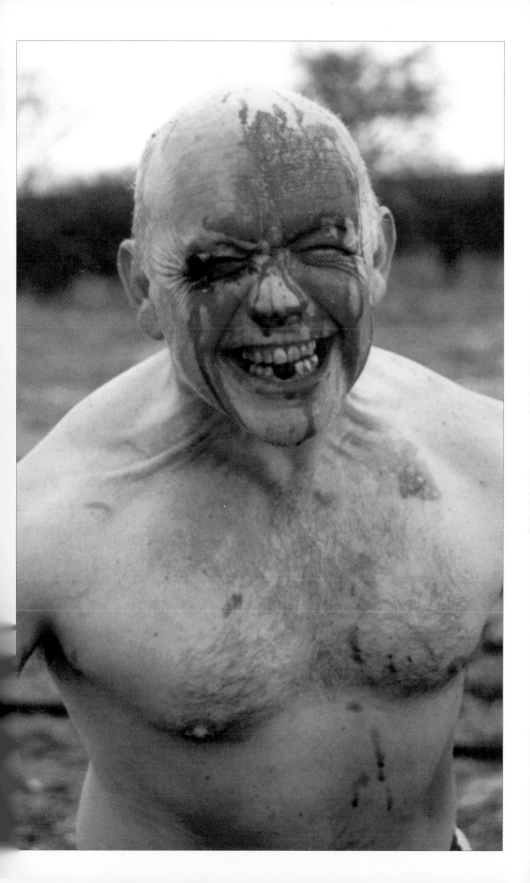

Reggie Parker, one of the toughest security men in the business.

Lonsdale Belt in the legitimate ring. In years gone by, every town or village fair would hold bare-knuckle contests and whoever won the most fights in that year at that fair would hold the title of The Guv'nor for the next 12 months.

There was no way that the young, strong, athletic Billy Cribb would not grow up trying his luck at bare-knuckle fighting. From his childhood memories, he can recall watching members of his family taking part in contests and, understandably, he couldn't wait to become involved in that world of tough, strong men and hard-fought contests. The fact that the young Billy also saw men being battered to the ground, many with their faces beaten to a pulp, their noses split and with blood and sweat covering their bodies never seemed to put off the young firebrand.

Billy has never forgotten his first fight more than 30 years ago. He said, 'My first fight seemed to happen almost accidentally, really. I had been training and sparring with my dad for some years and I had learned a lot, but my dad didn't think I was yet ready to take on an experienced fighter. Then, one day, a young and inexperienced lad, aged about 18, challenged my dad to a fight but he knew it would be so one-sided he refused the challenge. To my dad, that was most unusual. He had a reputation for taking on anyone who threw down a challenge, even if the other fella was massive.

'My dad hit on an idea; the lad could fight me and, if he beat me, then my dad would accept the challenge. In fact, I knew my dad would take it easy with the young fella, just teach him a trick or two but not hurt him. It would be more of a lesson than a real fight. My dad was good like that.

'The morning of the fight, I enjoyed a really big breakfast and then rushed off to vomit it all up. But as I was preparing for the fight, invigorating myself, boosting my adrenalin, stimulating my nervous energy, I suddenly realised that I had a *fan-fucking-tastic* hard-on! It was extraordinary, but that happened every time I was preparing for a fight; first I would vomit and then the erection would follow.

'Stripped to the waist, I walked into the square formed from four chrome trailers and I saw the other lad approaching. We eyed each other for a few seconds but we were both keen to get started. There were no preliminaries, no bells, just a crowd of men roaring us on.

'First blood went to the other lad who came racing towards me like a rabbit from a burrow. He struck me a blow on the face but in that instant I realised that he had made his first mistake. He allowed me a few seconds to clear my head from that first thump. The other lad was some 6ft tall and because I was only about 5ft 4in he had the reach advantage. So I used my brain. I crouched low, making myself a small target, keeping my arms high, covering my face and my head, making it difficult to find the target and get in a hard punch. I was learning.

'I knew that my chance would come once I could get inside his guard and thump away. I just waited, bobbing and swerving, keeping away from his haymakers.

'Before the fight, our fathers had settled the rules of the contest. We had agreed on a "straightener"; there would be no dirty fighting, no kicking, biting or nutting. Then, all of a sudden, he comes at me and tried to nut me. But because he was so much taller than me he missed and toppled over, the mug. That was the opportunity I had been waiting for, and I let fly a crashing punch to his nose which exploded in front of my eyes.'

Billy Cribb had won his first fight. He was delighted. It was the beginning of a great career in the bare-knuckle world.

Cribb believes that he gained much of his natural strength and ability from sheer hard work, labouring with his extended family in the hop fields and apple orchards of southern England. Billy would work from dawn to dusk humping hundreds of boxes of harvested hops and fruit a day, often in driving wind and rain. It was hard work, it was tough work, but it hardened and strengthened his upper body. In fact, that natural training schedule over several years prepared Billy for his life in the ring. There was no need for the teenage Billy to do weights, skipping or running because his everyday work slowly and inexorably was producing a really fit, strong young man with masses of stamina.

And from a young age he learned to box, to defend himself and, more importantly, to attack with ferocity and determination. Those techniques he learned from his father, uncles and from friendly gypsies. He also learned to be fearless, working with his dad in the high branches of trees in the lucrative but dangerous job of tree-lopping.

His uncle, aided by friendly gypsies, worked on tactics for young Billy. They devised plans to ensure that he could win bare-knuckle fights against taller and stronger opponents despite his small stature. They knew that Billy should have been ruled out of the sport purely because of his size, but he was so keen and showed so much aptitude that they persevered. He was not to disappoint them, particularly as young Billy had no fear of his larger, taller, more powerful opponents in the ring.

He would say later, 'One trick they taught me was how best to overcome the height difference between me and my opponents which was usually some five or six inches. They taught me to work the arms, telling me to punch their arm muscles as often and as hard as possible which, in the end, makes it almost impossible for the boxer to lift his arms, let alone throw a hard punch with them. I tried it on many occasions and found it worked.

'They also taught me to start the fights by targeting the lower part of my opponent's body, his abdomen and then his stomach, tiring and exhausting him while working my way up to the man's head and face. By then, I had hoped to have exhausted the bloke so he hadn't got the strength to throw any hard punches. Luckily for me, those tactics worked well.'

A once-in-a-lifetime-break gave Billy Cribb the chance he needed to propel him into one of the stars of the bare-knuckle circuit and he took it with both hands. It happened by accident. Young Billy was laying tarmac with some of his uncles and decided to have a bite to eat in a roadside café. A group of truckers arrived and, while they were waiting for their food, began making offensive remarks about 'fucking pikeys'.

Cribb didn't take too kindly to anyone making such remarks about people who had become his close friends. Billy felt that his honour had been offended and waded into the well-built, overweight truckers.

Billy said later, 'There was a tear-up inside the café and there was claret everywhere. Glass sauce bottles were used as weapons against me and my mates but we quickly knocked shit out of the hefty, slow-moving truckers. They scarpered.'

Unknown to Billy, however, a man by the name of Donny Adams, a hard man among bare-knuckle fighters, was in the café that day and he saw the professional manner with which Billy dealt with the truckers. Donny was so impressed with the speed with which Billy dispatched the hefty men that he contacted a fight manager by the name of Benny Harris.

Harris decided to take his exciting new prospect on to a new circuit based around the network of motorway service stations and A-road cafés across Britain. Billy said, 'I was in my twenties and raring to go. This seemed a great opportunity, especially when Harris christened me "The Tarmac Warrior". I loved that title.'

His first fight under his new name took place on a patch of concrete in a desolate corner of the Blue Boar motorway service station off the M1 near Northampton. Billy said later, 'Before the fight, I was tense, wanting the fight to be successful and not wanting to let down my new manager. This was an exciting period for me and I knew it was vital to my entire future to win that first fight. I was steaming before the fight and my aggression was really high. I felt great.

'I had been pitched against a well-built trucker

nicknamed "Tattoo" and I could see why. Most of his body was covered with tattoos. I thought the fight might be difficult because I hadn't heard anything about Tattoo and he looked well-built, capable of throwing a really hard punch. But in those few minutes before we came to blows, I thought he looked a bit overweight and I guessed he wasn't as fit as me. Thank goodness it turned out I was right. I adopted my low technique to make myself a difficult target and, whenever an opportunity arose, I went in hard. He went down after about five minutes with a good right hook. I had made it. I felt so relieved. That victory made me feel more confident and I felt that Benny would be happy to pitch me into more fights.'

Billy was gob-smacked when they returned to Benny's trailer that night. Benny threw Billy a fat wad of notes. He was amazed to discover that that first fight had netted him £1,000. Billy was hooked.

As a result, the young Billy began a nomadic life, travelling all over the British motorway network in search of contests and bare-knuckle fighters prepared to take him on. After that first successful fight Billy struck a deal with his manager. Benny Harris paid all Billy's expenses in return for half the purse and all the lucrative side-bets, a share of which Billy was also offered.

Billy recalled what happened in lorry parks the length and breadth of Britain. 'I was happy to take on all-comers, not caring a damn about their size or weight or reach. I was learning fast, learning how to handle the big, tall fellas and learning how to deal with them. Many fellas agreed to take me on after seeing the size of me, especially the big, heavyweight bastards who thought I would crumple after one haymaker. They were the guys, many inexperienced, who fancied a crack at bare-knuckle fighting when they saw how small I was. They were happy to throw in a good purse – winner takes all – because they could see easy money. But they were mistaken.

'All these fights were at the hard end of bare-knuckle fighting. There were no gloves, of course, and usually there was no ring, no bell, no referee, no rounds and no holds barred. I preferred "straighteners", but many of the newcomers fancied kicking, head-butting, biting, grappling, everything in fact. But I didn't win all those contests but I won enough to earn myself a damn good living.

'The fights would end only when one fighter couldn't go on any longer. The loser would say, "I'm done for, mate, I can't get up, you've fucking done me." And when a man said that, his opponent would immediately stop fighting. There was a code of honour and nearly everyone I ever fought abided by that code.'

However, Billy Cribb, The Tarmac Warrior, had to cut short his new-found career one day in a lay-by off the M62 near Manchester. Billy had been matched against 'Midnight', the nickname given to a black Brummie who practised the martial arts. A ring had been set up made from steel posts and rope surrounded the ring. The fight had only been in progress a few minutes and neither man had established a superiority, when a shout went up among the crowd of about 200 men who had come to see the fight.

'Police, police, run for it,' someone shouted. Billy

and the Brummie heard the warning and stopped fighting. Billy later explained what happened.

'Benny had been put away some time earlier for staging bare-knuckle matches and he knew that if he was caught again he would be facing a long stretch inside. He didn't want that, neither it seemed did any of the 200 men watching the fight.

'It seemed the two policemen had stumbled on the fight by accident. There was no raid as such. The two officers saw a crowd had gathered and heard the cheering and went over to investigate, to see what was happening. They were as surprised as anyone to find a bare-knuckle fight going on in a motorway car park.

'All hell broke loose. Benny screamed at me to run like hell, fearing we would both be facing time inside if we didn't make good our escape. Midnight's minders also realised the danger their man was in and he, too, was told to run to a car and escape.

'We were the lucky ones. The fellas watching the fight all realised they had to help us escape because we would be the ones in the shit so, as a mob, they turned on the two officers. In fact, the spectators were just doing their damnedest to protect me and Midnight but it seems things got out of hand. Some of them went a bit overboard; one officer ended up with horrific facial damage and the other was speared with a metal stake through the guts. That wasn't very pretty either.

'Benny and I, Midnight and his managers leapt into our cars and raced from the scene. And I was led to understand that the vast majority, if not all, of the spectators also escaped after making sure the coppers were in no fit condition to make any arrests. I heard later that the two coppers recovered from their injuries, thank goodness.'

So devastating were the injuries inflicted on the two Old Bill that a huge police hunt was launched in a bid to find, charge and convict anyone attending that fight, particularly the organisers and the two fighters. Benny thought he and Billy should lie low for a while to let the storm of protest and police anger and fury die down. So the two men took to the cross-channel ferries to earn a crust. In the winter months, with few travellers on board, bare-knuckle fights were organised in the dank cargo decks in the bowels of the ferries. But the takings weren't good. To begin with, Billy found himself earning only £50 a fight, usually against some drunk trucker who fancied having a go, not realising that Billy was a professional who knew how to dispatch such men in double-quick time.

But the word spread.

Truckers from Germany, France, Italy and Holland heard of the British bare-knuckle fighter, who was only 5ft 8in tall, taking on all-comers on cross-channel ferry trips. They heard that fights were arranged on board and came to watch them and, more importantly, to have a bet on the outcome. Within a few months, Billy and Benny began receiving challenges from truckers of other nationalities and the interest suddenly took off.

Dramatically, all the truckers began to see the fights as international boxing contests and pride in their nation began to play a part. Before long, Billy came to realise that he was now representing Britain, fighting for his country like any other boxer. No longer was it The Tarmac Warrior fighting some other nonentity, but the bare-knuckle contests became real internationals; England v Germany or England v Holland. As a result, the fights became more intense, the rivalries more acute, the various nationalities turning up in their hundreds to cheer on their countryman. The bare-knuckle fight game had become a real spectator sport on the ferries.

And the money began to roll in.

Some of the trans-continental truckers were happy to pay their fight purse with goods stolen from their vehicles. Benny was happy to take anything as long as he could sell it on after they had left the ferry at the end of the journey. On one occasion, they walked off the ship with two sheep they had won in a fight!

But the greater the interest, the more the purses began to escalate. After a few months, Benny and Billy were earning £2,000 for a good international fight which attracted big crowds and big side-bets. Good times were rolling again and Billy's reputation had spread across the continent wherever truckers gathered. Everyone spoke of the power and the punching of the short Brit who could punch shit out of the biggest and toughest truckers. The more the word spread about the champion Brit, the more powerful his opponents became. Billy was enjoying his life but he had to train and work hard at it. Sometimes, of course, he did take a bit of a battering and he would have to dig deep to beat some of the big fellas against whom he was pitted. But he kept winning and his reputation soared.

But Benny became money-mad. The man who had earned so much from Billy's fists, who had acquired so much money while Billy took the punches and the pain, was determined to earn as much money as possible from Billy's talent and bravery.

Billy explained what happened. 'Of course, I sometimes got injured, badly injured. But when you're in a real fight you don't immediately feel the pain because of the adrenalin surging through your body. On one occasion, a German bastard grabbed my head and repeatedly smashed my face down on one of the bars that hold the continental trailers together. My mouth was a crimson pulp, a mass of ripped flesh, and half my front teeth had gone. But at the time I hardly felt it because of the adrenalin.

'But even the adrenalin couldn't mask the horrific pain when a German bastard got hold of a compass spike and drove it deep into my calf muscle. Of course, that was against the rules of the match and I didn't see it coming. The pain was unbelievable, shooting straight up my leg. Of course, that injury was so horrendous that I had to throw in the towel. I couldn't even walk let alone move around a ring and defend myself.

'But a worse shock was to follow. To my horror, I discovered that the match had been a fix. Worse still, I found out that some of the guys I had trusted for so long had fixed the fight. They had also given the compass spike to the German and told him where to jam it into my leg knowing full well that such an injury would lose me the fight. Before the fight, those bastards had gone around everyone on board and bet them that the German would win that fight. They had picked up thousands!

'I was absolutely devastated, gutted. I couldn't believe that the guys I had fought for could do something like that to me. I was the guy who had risked my fucking life.'

Billy, a man of honour and principle, went to his room, packed a small bag and left behind everything he couldn't carry. When he got to the door to leave, his betrayers offered him half the winnings – but Billy didn't want to know. 'Shove it up your arse,' he spat and walked out.

Fed up with the whole fight game, Billy hitched a ride on an articulated lorry and headed for Spain, with the idea of resting, recuperating, relaxing and enjoying himself in Majorca's 'Shagaluf'. It was the start of another chapter in his remarkable life. He threw himself wholeheartedly into a hectic life enjoying an entire summer of sun, sand and sex. The English, German, Dutch and Scandinavian girls fell for the strongly built, powerful and muscular body Billy had to offer and he revelled in the carefree life.

After a while his funds dried up and Billy needed to earn a crust. A nightclub owner quickly hired him as a bouncer and he would happily carry out other work where a strong man, who could use his fists, might be needed. One night, a bunch of expatriate hoods invited him along as a guest to see a bare-knuckle fight. As he watched the fight, old memories came flooding back.

Later, Billy explained what happened. 'I suddenly felt that old rush of adrenalin again, the lure of the fight game. In the excitement of the evening, I jumped into the ring and ripped off my shirt. I shouted to everyone in the audience, "I'll fight any man for a grand!"

'I walked round the ring challenging some bloke to have a go but there seemed to be no takers. An

American got to his feet and shouted back, "I'll add another two grand to that!"

'That excited me. I waited in the ring for someone to respond, hoping someone would accept the challenge so that I could earn £2,000. I was certain I could beat anyone in the audience that night.

'To my delight, a Geordie named Makka, who also worked as a bouncer, jumped into the ring, keen to pick up the biggest pay-day of his career. We moved round for a minute or so, eyeing each other, and then – crack! – he caught me on the forehead. Then I put together a nice combination throwing him backwards.

'Makka came back at me with a flourish of poorly aimed punches. I could tell he was angry and wasn't thinking straight. His blows were hard and fast but not making any real contact while deliberately I remained calm and focused. That is one of the great secrets of good bare-knuckle fighters. The successful ones never lose their cool, never get angry or emotional but remain calm and focused on the job in hand.

'Donny Adams had taught me how to become a successful fighter, emphasising time and again that brain over brawn is the defining ingredient in any bare-knuckle fight.

'I waited patiently and then saw the opportunity I wanted. His guard was down and I went in hard, aiming for his nose. My fist made contact and his nose exploded, spurting claret everywhere. That sent shock waves through Makka, however, and he calmed down, realising that wild punches never won any fight. He began to out-think and out-punch me and I was worried.

'Makka came towards me, and I intended to side-step him and counter-punch. But he anticipated my move and brought his knee up sharply, smashing it into my left side. I went down with the pain. My side hurt like hell but it was only later that I discovered that his knee had cracked a rib and punctured a lung. I was now fighting on only 50 per cent breathing capacity and pure adrenalin.

'As I came up to face him again, he came down with his nut. I stumbled backwards and ripped off some of the tape covering my knuckles. I moved round the ring backwards, fumbling with the tape as I tried to tie some round my head to stop the flow of blood which I knew would soon pour into my eyes, blinding me. If that happened I was finished, and I wanted that £2,000.

'I managed to clear my head but knew that I had to finish this fight as quickly as possible if I was not to lose. My breath was coming in fits and starts but somehow I managed to trade blow for blow with the Geordie. We were both using everything in our repertoire, desperate to get the edge, to win the fight. We were both punching and kicking each other, using knees and elbows and heads; anything to gain the advantage. He was proving a really tough, rough customer and I was having to think fast just to keep in the fight.

'Then, after one punching–kicking sequence, we both fell to the canvas. We rose to our knees and continued trading punches, trying to smash the other man in the face. Blood was everywhere, all over the canvas. We were both bleeding from our noses, heads and faces. The crowd were screaming, many on their feet yelling for whoever they wanted to win.

'As we knelt on the canvas, Makka lurched forward and sank his teeth into my shoulder causing a searing pain to shoot down my arm. But I had seen my chance, my best chance that night. I grabbed his head and pulled it into my face ripping off the tip of his nose. The blood shot out and I knew that must have hurt like hell. But it made him break off. We managed to stagger to our feet but I now had a target – that battered nose, or what was left of it. I cupped my right hand and lifted it hard under what remained of his nose. That stopped him in his tracks. He let out a horrendous scream and brought both his hands over his face in agony.

'Now I knew I had him but he wasn't finished yet. I delivered one more vicious punch to the body, a straight-fingered blow under his ribs with all the force I could muster. He spun round in agony not knowing whether to shield his nose or his body. I knew that he was now in real pain. So in I went, thumping a left and then a right to his head in a last desperate attack to put an end to the fight. It worked. He went down, hitting the canvas with a thump. He was out cold.'

Those privileged to see that long, hard bare-knuckle fight believe it was one of the best examples of the art of no-holds-barred fighting they had ever seen in their lives. For years afterwards, those who witnessed the epic battle talked about it, always speaking with great respect for Billy Cribb and Makka who had both given everything that night.

An American in the audience at Gran Canaria that night immediately offered Billy a bare-knuckle fight in New York. But first, Billy had to recover from the battering his body, his head and his organs had suffered. His lung had to heal and so did all the grazes, the butchered skin and the bruises which covered his entire body. That had been one of Billy's most dramatic fights and he had won despite the fact that the fight came at the end of a lazy summer when he had done little except lie in the sun, swim in the warm waters and enjoy long nights of wild sex in the arms of countless girls.

In New York, Billy agreed to fight under the name of 'The Gypsy Prince' because he quickly learned that the great majority of Americans hated gypsies and he was happy to assume that persona. It only made him more determined to knock as much hell as possible out of American fighters, knowing they would squirm at the sight of the prime of American manhood being battered by a gypsy.

He found a manager by the name of Jerry who agreed to pay all of Billy's hotel bills and his living expenses in New York, in return for half the purse and half the side-bets. But Billy didn't like the mean streets of New York. 'The crowds were very aggressive and very anti me,' he explained. 'They always wanted me to lose and to get a real battering simply because they believed I was a gypsy. If I was being beaten in a fight, they yelled and screamed for my opponent to knock hell out of me. If I was winning, the crowds grew quiet. That was really shitty. It took the fun out of the whole business. I found I wasn't enjoying the fight game as I had done in Britain. The New York fight scene was a mean, contemptible, shitty scene and I didn't like it. The only pleasure I had was in knocking fuck out of the shits.'

Then, one day, Billy was stepping into the ring for a no-holds-barred, bare-knuckle fight in New York when a claw hammer came flying through the air. It hit Billy on the left temple, knocking him spark out. Apparently, the motive for the attack was revenge. Friends of a fighter Billy had really sorted out, injuring him in the process, wanted to settle the score. They couldn't find anyone game enough to take on Billy in the ring; they were too scared to do that. So they hammered him instead. His assailant disappeared in the 500-strong throng leaving Billy with a fractured skull.

Billy's handlers took him to a private New York hospital where he was smuggled into the place through the back door. It took him five long months to completely recover. And he's still got the round indentation on his head to this day.

Once again, Billy was to suffer at the hands of his manager. After the hammer blow, Billy decided he wanted to get the hell out of New York and get back to a more civilised life in Britain. But Jerry, his manager, told him he couldn't travel as he had lost his passport and needed to go through the whole process of getting him another one. Billy waited and waited and began fighting once again. More importantly, he started winning again and the money came rolling in. But Billy wasn't happy.

By chance, one day he discovered that his manager had possession of his passport all along and had deceived Billy so that he would have to stay longer in America earning them both a very nice living. Once again, Billy felt let down by someone he had trusted. But this time he was going to take his revenge, so as

Jerry helped Billy put his gear in the boot of his car one day, Billy took the golden opportunity of smashing the lid of the boot down on Jerry's hands. He broke the bones in the little hustler's hands and said goodbye.

Before long, Billy found himself back in America, but this time living in California where he felt far more relaxed and confident. But then disaster struck. The inexperienced, naïve, honest Billy got hooked on drugs – first dexedrine and then cocaine.

He also became involved in the Californian form of bare-knuckle fighting which the Americans then called 'extreme' or 'reality' fighting which is now known as 'Ultimate Fighting'. It is now a semi-respectable sport shown live on cable TV across the United States.

Most of the fights were held in the Nevada desert close to the state line so that if the cops ever showed up everyone would simply bolt across the state line out of the jurisdiction of the Californian police departments.

Billy discovered that this new style of fighting, which was similar to bare-knuckle boxing, became the favourite spectator sport of the movie stars at that time. Celebrities such as Marlon Brando, Paul Newman and Jack Nicholson would fly in by helicopter to watch the modern-day gladiators strutting their stuff.

But it was wild action. On one occasion, Billy found himself fighting hanging upside down or tied by the ankles to his opponent. Queer, odd, and stupid was Billy's view of such proceedings. Billy was once persuaded to fight in a giant perspex tank; on another occasion, he fought in a grain silo with sand pouring over him throughout the fight. It was all spectacle, all hype, all crap, all nonsense. And all the time the charlie was being poured into him whenever he fancied it. To him and some of the other fighters, the coke was all free. Bags of it, as much as they wanted, whenever they wanted.

Billy continued this drug-crazy life for three years; fighting the weird fights, winning most but losing some and always, but always, stoned on coke. It ruled his life and he hated it. But life was easy, the money came and went and his life was passing him by in a drug-induced cloud of unreality.

Then he was shaken out of his dream world by the most terrible event. A mate of Billy's, a black bare-knuckle fighter by the name of Berry who had also been seduced by the free cocaine, died from terrible internal injuries following a fight. Berry had been like a father-figure to Billy but the drugs and the fight-game had destroyed him, totally. At the time, Berry was also deranged by coke, hardly able to differentiate between reality and false, floating dreams. His mate's death hit Billy hard and made him sit up and think what the fuck he was doing with his life. Once again he walked out, not knowing where he was going or what he would do.

He said later, 'I had to escape. Something inside my head told me that I had to escape now or I, too, would end up dead just like my poor mate. I then realised the full horror of what the Americans had been doing to me and the others, drugging us like fuck so that we would agree to any of their stupid demands. They were earning good money out of me and the other fighters and stupidly we thought we were living in seventh heaven. But the laugh was on us. In reality, we were living only half-lives in real shit but I had been too stupid to realise what the fuck had been going on. The fact that, drugged and only half-conscious, we could still fight and not feel most of the pain must have helped.'

He went to Carmel on the Californian coast still in his own private drug-induced dream world and sat on the beach looking out across the Pacific and he thought of Cornwall and good old Blighty. Carmel became a sort of second home to Billy, where he met a beautiful teenager by the name of Sweetness, an angelic Jesus-freak. Billy fell in love with his young angel and she, in turn, converted Billy to a life dedicated to Jesus and born-again, happy-clappy Christianity.

Billy commented, 'The Jesus thing saved my sanity and probably my life. Sweetness taught me to respect myself and, because of her, I kicked the drugs and spent my life loving her and making love to her. I was hooked, in love, and slowly the drugs lifted from my mind and my body and I got my life back into some sort of shape.'

Then, devastation. He discovered that in this culture of free-love which Sweetness had taken on board, she was free to go and screw anyone else she fancied. For Sweetness, there were no ties; all was free love. If she fancied another man for a night, for a screw, then she went for it. Sometimes Sweetness screwed Billy, at other times she would screw the new man in her life. To her, it made no difference for she was free to share her body with anyone. But Billy couldn't hack it. He was in love with the girl and he couldn't take another man screwing his darling Sweetness. So, once again, he packed his bags and this time he headed for the airport and a flight back home to England. His

American nightmare was over.

Back home in England he was reunited with all his huge family and they were glad Billy was back in their midst. But Billy had had enough of bare-knuckle boxing. He had fought perhaps 1,000 fights and, in his mind, enough was enough. People came from far and wide to challenge The Tarmac Warrior but he didn't want to know.

But Billy still enjoyed the sport, attended fights, became a warm-up man telling jokes and stories and keeping the punters happy while they waited for the action to start. He also became deeply involved in helping the Romany families of Central Europe re-establish themselves after the Iron Curtain had finally crumbled and the eastern European nations had thrown off the shackles of Communism and the Soviet Union.

Ever since World War II, when the Nazis hunted, jailed and killed the gypsies of Europe in their hundreds of thousands as they did the Jews, nothing whatsoever had been done for them. The Communist regimes of eastern Europe ignored them, drove them from the cities, and exiled them to cope as best they could together. But the Romany peoples have lived under such conditions for centuries and always survived through their grit and determination, their honour and their traditions. Billy is now one of their foremost champions, working tirelessly for their rights, helping the ageing Romanys end their days in some comfort and working to bring a proper education to the Romany kids who are the future.

Another man responsible for encouraging gypsy families to take up the gauntlet and accept the challenges of the bare-knuckle brigade is Joey Pyle, a veteran of the fight game, both licensed and, more importantly, unlicensed. Joey Pyle earned the reputation as the man capable of organising and promoting fights anywhere in Britain with some of the best fighters. He not only knew everyone of note in the licensed fight game and the bare-knuckle world but had the respect of everyone to organise fights which weren't one-sided or fixed. He only had to pick up a phone and make a call and a fight would be organised. People always trusted Joey and he never betrayed that trust in the decades he was the fixer.

Joey Pyle is known throughout the underworld as the man nobody challenges, nobody touches. Joey knows everyone who matters in the jungle of Britain's most dangerous criminals and the vast majority of those men respect him as the Godfather.

For decades, the resourceful, quiet Joey Pyle has sorted out problems, everyone's problems. He is quiet and thoughtful and he knows when to act like a hard man and when to let sleeping dogs lie.

Joey Pyle, born in 1937, will soon officially become an old age pensioner, but his power and his authority still remain. Not for one moment is Joey thinking of retiring, hanging up his boots, taking life easily and keeping out of the limelight.

At the age of 18, Joey was tempted to start a life of crime. Some of his friends had decided on a bit of villainy and they had told him of the opportunities which presented themselves, rather than spending their entire life working 9-to-5, five days a week, for very little return. Joey decided to take the plunge and followed in their footsteps. And his baptism into the life of crime was extraordinary.

He had been told that a Territorial Army headquarters was stuffed with money so he decided to investigate. To his astonishment, he discovered the TA safe contained £7,000! So he helped himself to the lot. In the late 1950s, when the average wage was only £12 a week, that sum of money was an absolute fortune. Joey never looked back.

But despite his undoubted intelligence, Joey did sometimes fall foul of the law. He was arrested 50 times and judges sentenced him to some 35 years in jail. He was tried at the Old Bailey in the famous Court Number One four times for murder, robbery and drug smuggling. But on each of those occasions he was found 'not guilty'.

But he enjoyed his life. He found a life of crime a great challenge, keeping one step ahead of the law whenever possible. He knew that he was taking risks but he found carrying out those risks gave him a great boost of adrenalin. He thrived on the excitement and the narrow scrapes. He loved living dangerously. He also enjoyed planning his life of crime, recce'ing scenes of the crime, plotting and planning, using his undoubted intelligence to keep out of trouble.

Throughout his life of crime, Joey actually spent a total of 15 years behind bars always being released early because of his good behaviour. As Joey put it, 'I was determined to do whatever was necessary to get out of jail as quickly as possible. So I decided to behave myself and get out quickly. To me, that was the only way to play the game, and win. It also meant that I could enjoy my life.'

Many criminals came to Joey for advice, and some still do. Joey would check over their plans, offer his advice, sort out the best methods of carrying out some villainy and, on most occasions, the villains would adopt his plans knowing that Joey's advice was always sound.

Joey Pyle also enjoyed the world of bare-knuckle fighting. Many of the great bare-knuckle boxers came to Joey asking him to promote fights, organising them and setting up contests between the fighters. Organising bare-knuckle fights had to be done secretly, of course, because such contests were against the law. He would not only find the right opponent for someone but would also find the venue and make sure that only those who could keep their months shut would be invited.

He also contacted those bookies who wanted to take bets on the outcome of such fights for, in bare-knuckle contests, nearly every punter lays a bet on whom they believe will be the victor. Many bookies, most of them unlicensed, made small fortunes on bare-knuckle fights.

In his younger days, Joey had tried his hand at legitimate boxing. His dad's twin brother Joe was the ABA Amateur Welterweight Champion of Great Britain and, as a child, he would watch his uncle with admiration and enthusiasm. Joey himself began boxing at the age of 12 at the Angel in Islington.

Joey proved a natural boxer, helped by advice from his uncle Joe. Joey himself was strong and powerful for his age with a very good, hard punch. He learned from an early age to put all his weight into a punch which was responsible for many quick victories inside the distance.

Joey Pyle won loads of trophies and eventually he became the schoolboy boxing champion of Surrey.

He decided to turn professional and earn a living from the legitimate, licensed ring. By the age of 18, Joey was a well-built, powerful, athletic young men, 6ft 2in tall and weighing 13 stone. However, he lost his very first professional fight and discovered that he needed to train harder, get fitter and undertake more sparring matches to increase his speed and his skill.

In all, he won 20 fights, some against really tough opposition, but he enjoyed the fight game. He liked many of the professional fighters he met and he took a pride in keeping superbly fit. He also met some young men who were enjoying life on the wrong side of the law and he listened to their lives of thrills and danger.

It wasn't long before Joey heard about the TA safe filled with cash and, from that moment, his life changed completely. He abandoned the fight game and concentrated on a life of crime. He believed he could earn far more following a life of villainy than enjoying the hard life in the world of boxing.

Joey has remained close to the bare-knuckle fight game for many years but he didn't fancy getting personally involved, although many tempted him to have a go. But Joey had a problem. He had been trained as a boxer, an amateur boxer who fought within the rules of the sport. But he also saw many a bare-knuckle fight in which there were no rules; nothing was barred.

Joey had been present at the roughest, toughest bare-knuckle fights staged in Britain over the past 30 years. He had witnessed at close quarters the terrible damage that was sometimes inflicted on those fighters; eyes gouged out, hair torn out, testicles ferociously squeezed, boots repeatedly smashed into people's stomachs and faces, noses split in two, mouths ripped open, teeth knocked out and faces and necks bitten and torn apart.

He was sensible enough to realise that having never entered the shadowy world of bare-knuckle fights, where anything and everything goes, he would find such a dramatic change very, very difficult. So, instead of participating, he organised the fights. Joey Pyle became one of the great organisers and, in doing so, he won respect.

And there was another side to Joey.

For most of the time, Joey was quiet, at times completely silent, keeping his thoughts and his opinions to himself. He was an intelligent man, a thinker who only spoke when he had some sound advice to give. He never shot off his mouth, never boasted of his deeds or his contacts. But Joey had a way of making things happen. And that won him tremendous respect.

And Joey learned to be a diplomat. He learned when to be gentle, which was not very often, but more importantly, he learned when to be tough. He could be kind, gentle and understanding; he could also be utterly ruthless and brutal, merciless and implacable.

Joey could talk to anyone and feel at home with them. He had the capability to mix in any circle whether it was with members of parliament, celebrities or murderers. He listened before spouting off his views and never liked to offer advice until he knew all the facts.

Even senior police officers, who knew Joey Pyle to be king of the villains, had respect for him because they knew he was highly intelligent. In his way, Joey was also honest. Of course, he was a law-breaker but he dealt with people honestly.

'If you've got a problem, go and see Joey Pyle,' was the word in London's vast network of criminals, 'he'll sort it out for you.'

And he did.

Some people treated Joey as the criminal's favourite lawyer, though, of course, he wasn't a lawyer. But he had experience of the law, tons of it, and criminals would come to him for legal advice and, more often than not, he would be able to offer them sound advice.

Perhaps his best piece of advice was the principle he had lived by throughout his life – a still tongue keeps a wise head. He knows that far too many villains try to talk their way out of trouble, only to find later that much of what they said was used against them.

'If you don't say anything, no one can argue with you,' he has often said with a wry smile. 'Keeping silent can often save many a man from a long prison sentence.'

CHAPTER 9

At the age of 18, young 'Cracker' Stone found himself in trouble with the law. His older brother Jack was about to be married and Cracker wanted to buy him a really good present. But he was skint, stoney broke, and the money he was earning from bare-knuckle fights had all but gone.

As he explained later, 'I decided to "borrow" some. I heard that a lorry-load of booze was being delivered around the Newcastle area and that, for one night, the lorry would be parked in a certain lorry park on the edge of the city. The lad driving the vehicle happened to be a mate of mine and he told me that for that one night he would not be sleeping in the cab but at a guest house where he had a long-standing romantic arrangement with the landlady. Whenever he visited

Newcastle, this landlady gave him a bed for the night and a good, hearty bacon and egg breakfast in return for favours.'

But as Cracker was driving the vehicle away to a warehouse to unload the booze, he was stopped by police. He had no driving licence and no proof that he was employed by the firm delivering the booze. The police nicked him and the following day he was in court on half-a-dozen charges all relating to taking and driving away the vehicle and stealing £20,000 worth of spirits. Luckily for Cracker, he was given bail.

Young Cracker discussed the problem with his folks and they reckoned he would be banged up for about five years because it wasn't exactly the first time he had fallen foul of the law. He decided to flee the country and, after staying away for some years, he would consider returning home. He was single and fancy free with no children and no responsibilities. The family bought him a one-way air ticket to Sydney, Australia, and gave him the names of Romany families who had moved down-under years before. They also gave him a few quid. Cracker was away.

The fresh-faced young man stepped off the plane at Sydney Airport not knowing what he would do or where he would live. He had very little with him except the clothes he arrived in and a few personal items, as well as some T-shirts and a spare pair of jeans his brother had given him as a going away present. Fortunately, it was summer and the weather was hot, the skies blue and the sea inviting.

The only place Cracker had heard about was Bondi Beach, so he caught a bus straight there from the airport carrying all his worldly possessions in three plastic supermarket bags. He was stunned by what he saw as soon as he stepped off that bus and on to the beach; scores of beautiful, bikini-clad girls walking around and sunbathing on the golden sands. To Cracker, Bondi seemed like paradise.

He said later, 'I thought I had arrived in heaven. It seemed so different to England where it had been cold and raining when I left. I had never seen so many beautiful girls in one place in my life.'

For seven days and nights, Cracker lived on Bondi Beach and slept there, too. He survived on beef burgers, meat pies and chips, shaved in the gents' lavatories and washed his T-shirts and jeans in the sea! But the little money he brought with him wasn't going to last long. He had to find work and he had to earn a living. He also had to think seriously about finding somewhere to live because he realised he couldn't live on the beach for ever. He also understood that, even in Sydney, the winters could be cold and wet.

He toured the pubs around Bondi Beach asking if there were any vacancies for bar staff. The first two turned him down because he had no experience and he wasn't yet familiar with the Australian currency, dollars and cents. The third hired him as a casual waiter, cleaning and clearing the tables on the terrace outside the pub. He knew the pay was lousy but he had no choice.

During the day, the pub was frequented mainly by young people and by wives wanting a day sunbathing. By night, the heavy mob moved in, the truckers, wharfies and labourers who were *real* Australian drinkers, throwing back the schooners as though there was no tomorrow. He noted that, at night, there was hardly a woman present in the pub, just men. In the morning, the market men dropped by after their work humping baskets and cases. Cracker was happy to work morning, noon and night and he continued to sleep on the beach.

One night, a couple of wharfies who had had too much to drink began throwing punches over some silly argument. Two minutes later, the entire place had erupted with punches and beer glasses being thrown all over the place and people thumping the fuck out of each other. Cracker kept out of the way, not wanting to become involved in a wild free-for-all when he had no idea whose side he should be on. But that fight made him itch to have another crack at bare-knuckle fighting. And the opportunity would come sooner than he thought.

A few nights later, a big, fat trucker, probably around 30 years of age and weighing some 15 stone, began making insulting remarks about Cracker, calling him 'a Pommie fairy'. Cracker took exception to the remark but kept his cool and walked away. But the Aussie trucker sensed he was right and followed Cracker, taunting him, challenging him to come outside and prove he wasn't a 'Pommie poofter'. Six times or more Cracker told him to 'Shut up' and 'Go away' so that he could get on with his work.

When the bar had closed and Cracker was mopping the tables and the terrace, the Aussie trucker and two mates walked back to him and began pushing Cracker around, shoving him in the chest, in the back, taunting him to have a go. They pushed him once too often but Cracker kept his cool.

When the shitty trucker moved towards him again, Cracked smashed him on the point of the jaw with all his force and followed that with a left and a right to the head. The trucker reeled backwards, stumbled and fell. One of his other mates ran towards Cracker but Cracker side-stepped the bastard and crashed an upper-cut on to his chin as he tumbled towards him. He also went down. The third bastard froze on the spot and, as Cracker moved towards him, he turned and fled.

The following night the pub manager called Cracker into his office. In his broad Aussie accent, he said, 'I saw what you did last night. You're nifty with your fists.'

Cracker said nothing, wondering what was coming next.

'I've been thinking,' he went on, 'things are getting a bit out of hand around here and I need someone who can look after himself and take care of the others if some of the heavy drinkers turn nasty. I'm thinking I might offer you the job. Do you fancy it?'

'A bouncer?' Cracker suggested.

'Yeah, sort of,' replied the boss.

Cracker thought fast. 'How much a week?'

'You're on the basic now working all God's hours. I'll give you three times your current pay to work nights only. You can do what you like during the day but you have to be fit and on the ball at night, every night.'

'Seven nights a week,' said Cracker.

'No, six will do,' he said. 'We never have any trouble on a Sunday night. And, by the way, no drinking on the job. OK?'

'Done,' said Cracker and they shook hands.

Cracker Stone had arrived in Australia and got himself a well-paid job. He felt good. He also felt pretty confident that he could handle the Aussie locals, especially if they were pissed before turning troublesome.

Fortunately for Cracker, he had an old head on his young shoulders and he knew this new job might not be the piece of cake he hoped for. He was quite fit but not fight fit and that was his first target. Every day he ran on the beach, swam miles in the seas off Bondi and volunteered to do portering in the markets. He carried heavy baskets and full packing cases around the place all morning, building his muscles and increasing his stamina. The part-time porter's job also earned extra dollars.

Cracker found himself a tiny flat in King's Cross, the heart of Sydney's red-light district. The place had a kitchenette, a shower room and a studio room with a sofa bed, small table and two chairs. It was also bloody hot in the summer and Cracker had to sleep with the doors and the windows wide open.

Before long, Cracker became friendly with some of the girls who worked in the immediate area and three who rented rooms in his small block.

He said later, 'I realised what was going on about 24 hours after moving in. I refused the girls' offers though I did fancy a couple of them. In fact, I became quite friendly with a few of them, especially the ones who used the rooms in my block. They were all young and trying to earn a crust. But I didn't want to get involved because I presumed they all had pimps and I knew those bastards would cut my throat if they thought I was trying to muscle in on their territory.'

Back at the big, barn-like pub where he worked as the bouncer, Cracker was quickly on nodding terms with the heavy drinkers who visited the place pretty well every evening. The landlord had told his regulars that Cracker was sharp with his fists and that he would be around in case of trouble.

One night, some four weeks or so after taking the job, about half-a-dozen rugby league supporters came in having obviously had a few beers beforehand. They were all loud-mouths and seemingly half-pissed, spilling their beers which they ordered three at a time and touring the other bars in the pub looking for girls. They came across two or three and tried, in their half-drunken state, to chat them up. A couple of them, all tough, well-built fellas, began asking one or two of the girls 'to come outside for a fuck'.

The landlord, who was named Billy, called over Cracker and told him to keep an eye on the six rugby supporters. Some of the regulars went to see Billy and asked him to order the trouble-makers off the premises.

Cracker took up the story. 'Billy asked me to go over with him to where the rugby supporters were causing a bother. He asked them to drink up and leave the pub because they had had enough. They told Billy to "Fuck off" and leave them alone. Two of the lads then went over to two girls and pulled them to their feet, grabbed them by the arms and began frog-marching them out of the pub. Billy intervened and told them to let go of the girls and leave. Once again they told him to "Fuck off" and mind his own business.

'Billy threatened to call the police and one fella threw a punch, catching Billy on the side of the head. I had seen enough and stepped in, grabbing the fella's arm and twisting it viciously behind his back in an arm-lock. I began to march him towards the door when two of his mates came rushing towards me, their fists in the air.

'I let go the fella's arm, hit the first thug a cracking right cross to the jaw and he fell back. The second took a swing and missed. I grabbed his arm and wrenched it as hard as I could over my shoulder. I heard it crack as he let out a scream of pain.

'Now, another two fellas came towards me and I knew the only chance was to try and take them out., The first looked really pissed so I chose him, cracked him with a left and a right to the head and then booted him in the stomach. The second caught my head with a haymaker and I reeled back with the shock and the force of the punch. Shit, I thought, this bastard can punch.

'By now, some of Billy's regulars had come to the rescue and a right old scuffle was taking place all around the bar. Girls were screaming and the fellas were throwing punches left and right. I heard Billy shout that he was calling the police and he disappeared. Then I really got stuck in. When I saw any of the six trouble-makers I belted them as hard as I could but they were pissed and didn't seem to feel my punches, but I knew they would in the morning!

'With the help of the regulars, we managed to get a grip on all six of the bastards and were marching them out of the pub when three police cars arrived. I left them to it. I had a few big bruises on my face and my knuckles hurt like hell, but otherwise I was OK.'

But it was not the end of the matter.

A week or so later, when Cracker had finished for the night, he was walking from the beach to his pad in King's Cross when a car pulled up alongside him. Three fellas leapt out of the car and began attacking him. 'We'll teach you to fuck with us, you Pommie bastard,' they shouted at him and began to land punches to the head and body. Cracker fought back as best he could but this time the three bruisers weren't pissed and they could all punch, hard. Cracker managed to fell one, butting him full in the face and splitting open his nose, the claret spurting everywhere and putting the bastard out of action. That enraged the other two and Cracker went down under a torrent of blows. As he fell to the ground, the two left standing put in the boot and then fled to their car and away.

Cracker got slowly to his feet and sat down on the pavement's edge while he checked his injuries, mopped the blood from his face and tried to clear his throbbing head. His ribs hurt like hell and he wondered if one or two might be cracked. His head felt as though it had been smashed into the ground a dozen times and he felt physically sick. A police car drove up and two cops got out. When they realised Cracker hadn't been drinking but had obviously been beaten up, they put him in the car and dropped him off at his block. He had told the cops that he was OK and didn't want to go to hospital. When he walked into the block, two of the young street girls saw the state of him and helped him upstairs.

Cracker spent the next two days at home recovering. And three of the street girls took turns getting him drinks and giving him whatever he needed to eat. When he got to the pub on the third day Cracker's face and his body were still badly bruised and one eye was half-closed. After listening to what had happened, Billy, the manager, sent him straight back home with a $200 bonus. 'You've earned that, mate,' Billy told him, 'you were fucking great the other night.'

Forty-eight hours later, Cracker was back at work and he had been given a good raise but he knew he didn't want to stay too long in that job. He planned to save money and then take off round Australia. But he hadn't reckoned with one of the girls who nursed him.

Francine was her name, a 19-year-old daughter of a Sydney prostitute who had been on the game since the age of 16. Francine was short, slight and quite pretty with blonde streaks in her short hair. She lived in a block next door and had brought Cracker cool drinks when he hadn't the strength to get out of bed.

They became lovers and Cracker found himself becoming protective towards this girl who seemed to worship him. She loved his muscles and his body and she liked the fact he hardly ever had a drink. She also liked Cracker chatting to her, treating her like a girlfriend, not someone on the game.

Cracker confessed later, 'Within a couple of weeks I had fallen for Francine. She was the first girl who had ever cared for me, cooked for me, washed and ironed my clothes and looked after me. We had fantastic sex together and I was convinced she loved me as I loved her. But I couldn't hack her fucking other guys for money though she promised me they always wore condoms. She told me the other fellas meant nothing to her; that being on the game was just a job like any other. She told me she never had an orgasm with any of her clients, though she pretended to.

'During those months together, I found out about women for the first time in my life. I began to fuck Francine all the time we were together, trying to shag her so much she wouldn't be able to fuck any of her clients. I even began to slip money into her purse so she would think she had more funds than she realised. She told me that I was fucking her brains out and that she was exhausted from having no sleep. I became some sort of fucking machine, driving myself to exhaust her. It worked for a while but I couldn't keep it up. After several weeks, I was absolutely shattered, working at the pub, portering and trying to satisfy Francine.

'I asked her to give up working as a prostitute but she told me she couldn't because she owed money to a pimp who moved between Melbourne and Sydney. To make matters worse, the pimp returned soon afterwards and although I pleaded with her to run away with me, to Brisbane, Perth, anywhere, she told me she could not do so because the pimp would just demand the money she owed from her mother.'

One night, as Cracker approached his block of flats, three men jumped him, slashing his face with a razor, cutting him down both cheeks from the eye to the chin. As he tried to protect himself he felt a terrible pain at the back of his head and blacked out. He awoke in hospital with Francine at the bedside telling Cracker that he must leave Sydney immediately otherwise he would be killed. She would be, too. Cracker's face was a mess with two huge scars down either side of his face. The following day he was allowed to leave hospital. He handed in his notice to Billy at the pub and he could see what had happened.

'If you ever want your job back again, just phone,' Billy told him. 'You've been a mate.'

Francine told Cracker to go and forget her; and maybe come back to see if she was still around in three or five years' time. He asked one last time for her to go with him but she just shook her head. 'I can't,' she whispered.

Cracker bagged up his possessions and took a coach to Brisbane, 500 miles up the coast in Queensland. In fact, he stopped off at Surfer's Paradise where the meter-maids walked around all day in bikinis politely telling people not to park their cars in restricted areas otherwise they *might* have to hand out a parking ticket. The sun was even hotter and Cracker was back in his own paradise for the place was full of gorgeous girls and hunky fellas from all over Australia enjoying their annual holidays.

Once again he found a job as a bouncer, this time in a holiday pub where he quickly learned that the young, sporty Aussie men couldn't hold their beer. Most nights he found himself escorting at least half-a-dozen sick, drunken young fellas out of the pub. But there was no real trouble.

Cracker's affair with Francine had given him a confidence with girls that he had never known before. Now he paid attention to them, joked and laughed with them and flirted with them. He was suntanned and fit again, though the scars on his face still showed red and raw which didn't enhance his dark complexion but did make a talking point. The scars also showed that he was a tough Pommie bastard who commanded respect.

One hundred miles inland from Brisbane, he heard that a fair, with a boxing ring, had come for its annual visit and would be staying for around one month. He thought of his old days back home and the yearning he had to follow in the family tradition and wondered if the ring encouraged bare-knuckle fights. He took a few days off work and hitched a lift in a cattle truck. The fair was pretty pathetic but that didn't bother him. He was only interested in the boxing ring but disappointed that the boxers had to wear gloves, although they were light 6oz gloves. He hung around and shook his head when the ringmaster asked him to step in and win $20 going a round with the resident boxer, a well-built, bald-headed fella around 40 years old, under 6ft tall and weighing about 15 stone. He looked mean but Cracker didn't think he was very fit.

He watched a few bouts in the evening and some were staged with the challengers walking away with $20 in their pockets. As the evening wore on and more Aussies drank more pints of beer, more challengers were keen to have a go. After seeing off seven or eight hopefuls and taking their money, the ringmaster upped the 'anti', offering $100 if anyone could put his man on the canvas. Three or four tried unsuccessfully, losing their $20 notes and when Cracker judged the time was ripe, he held up his $20 and jumped into the ring.

He later told what happened. 'I pulled on the gloves which had seen better days and noted that the boxer himself wore better, heavier gloves, giving him and me better protection from injury. We walked round eyeing each other and he flicked out a couple of punches. There were about 50 people mainly cheering for me because I was supposedly the underdog challenger. He caught me a couple of blows on the head, a left and a right which woke me up. I figured he could box but I sensed he was tired, not really trying because he reckoned he didn't have to. I hit him one hard shot in the stomach, which he didn't like, and when he crumpled forward hit him hard on the chin. He didn't like that either. I saw a change in his eyes. Now he began to take me seriously.

He hit me a couple of hard blows to the head and got through my guard, smashing one left on my nose. He stood back to see what effect those punches had made and, as he dropped his guard, I lunged forward, feinted with my right and delivered a ferocious uppercut with my left. His chin was totally unprotected and he reeled backwards, nearly falling to the canvas. He managed to hold on to the ropes, shook his head a couple of times and came towards me in a fury, swinging haymakers everywhere but not making contact. Suddenly, his face was right in front of me and I crashed a left straight on his nose, splitting it. Blood spurted all over the place and the cheers egged me on. He began to retreat and I followed, measuring my step and my punches, hitting him in the stomach and the face. He looked towards his corner and a towel was thrown into the ring. I had done it; won a $100 and had hardly been touched.'

However, Cracker was in for a surprise. The

ringmaster argued that as his man had not been put down on the canvas he could not give him the $100. Cracker had fallen for one of the oldest tricks in the game. He argued, he called on others for support but the ringmaster was adamant; the champ hadn't hit the canvas so there was no $100 prize, though he conceded Cracker had just about won the bout.

The following day, Cracker waited around the ring once more and again, late in the evening, he challenged for the $100 prize. His challenge was refused and the punters booed and hissed, catcalled and shouted obscenities. Cracker walked away, angry at the ringmaster and angry with himself for being so easily duped.

'Hey, Pommie.'

Cracker heard the call as he was drifting away from the fair. It was the ringmaster, the Master of Ceremonies who had cheated him out of $100.

'What do you want?' Cracker replied when he realised who had called him.

'Can I buy you a drink, mate?' said the MC.

'Why?' replied Cracker, 'What the fuck would I want a drink with you?'

'I wanna talk to you. I've got an offer.'

'Yeah?' Cracker replied, 'and what might that be?'

'It's for real, promise,' said the MC. 'Come on, you've got nothing to lose, I promise you.'

'Promise? Fuck off,' said Cracker and turned away.

But the MC wasn't finished yet. 'I wanna offer you a job.'

Cracker stopped. 'What job?'

'My champ's packing up, leaving. He didn't like the

way you hit him the other night. He's had enough. He's going back home. I want you to take his place.'

'I'll have that drink then,' replied Cracker, 'see what you've got to offer.'

An hour later, the MC was driving Cracker back to Surfer's Paradise in his car. Cracker had agreed to run with the fair, become their resident boxer. He was to be paid $100 a week all found, all expenses paid, and receive 50 per cent of the ring takings. The MC, whose name was Al, 'Big Al', promised there would be no fiddling. And from that moment Cracker would be called 'Scarface'. He couldn't argue with that!

Together Cracker and Big Al toured Australia with the fair, stopping in the small towns all over Queensland, New South Wales, Victoria and South Australia. They made most of their money, of course, when they pitched their fair in Brisbane, Sydney, Melbourne and Adelaide. That's when the punters threw their money around and Cracker had to look to his laurels to earn his money. But it was good money. He could earn $200 a night, $1,200 a week in the big cities. And he saved the lot.

Cracker became a great crowd-puller. He was young, well-built, reasonably handsome and bloody good with his fists. He was known as Cracker, the Scarface Pommie. Many of those who took him on wanted to do so because they all believed they could beat a Pommie with ease. Others just wanted the satisfaction of thumping a Pommie. Cracker didn't care a fuck as long as they showed up and put up the money.

Cracker said later, 'The more noses I split open, the more claret I spilled, the more the suckers queued to have a smack at me. Most of the time, it wasn't hard work, because the more I boxed, the more professional I became. I worked on my speed, side-steps, moves which confused the punters. Then I would hit them six or seven times, really hard, and the contest would be over.

'But on half-a-dozen occasions, I suppose, I relaxed too much and walked into trouble. I must have paid out $100 on six or seven occasions having been put on my back by a punter, usually some guy built like a brick shit-house who had one punch, a haymaker. I just hadn't been quick enough and he had caught me before I realised it. But if ever I was put down, the following night punters would be queuing to have a crack at me and we would take a small fortune.'

They had been on the road perhaps a year or so when, in a country town in New South Wales, Big Al came up with a proposition. A punter had asked whether he would put up $500 for a bare-knuckle purse if it was matched by another $500. Cracker would get all the money if he won, nothing if he lost. In any future bare-knuckle fights, Big Al would take fifty per cent of the purse.

That first night of bare-knuckle boxing, Cracker fought two men and won both fights. He pocketed $1,500. In his bank book Cracker now had the grand total of $25,000! He felt like a king but he told no one of his secret hoard of savings. He didn't even tell his girlfriend, the fair's trapeze artist named Mimi who was 18-years-old, only 5ft tall and weighed just 6 stone. Cracker became her protector and her lover and the two were inseparable. Friends in the fair urged them to marry, but Cracker didn't want to know. He didn't want the responsibility; he just wanted a girlfriend to share his bed.

Cracker was becoming quite a star down-under with his reputation preceding him in every town the fair pitched its tents. He was fast becoming the fair's great attraction as the young Aussie fellas were queuing up to fight him, desperate to try their luck against the Scarfaced Pommie. He was billed as the bare-knuckle boxer no one could beat. Such publicity brought the fair great notoriety and great rewards but it meant that when Cracker came to any town he could expect a queue of well-built lads wanting to knock his head off and, more importantly, put him on the canvas.

The Aussie lads were taking Cracker's success as an insult to Australian manhood that a Pommie could be so brilliant, so tough, so macho that not a single Aussie could put him on his back. Cracker was fortunate that bare-knuckle boxing had never been much of a craze in Australia since the days of the convict ships.

The convicts, ferried out in chains from England during the nineteenth century, had brought with them the rugged tradition of bare-knuckle fights. Once settled in Australia – and virtually devoid of womenfolk – one of the convicts' favourite sports was bare-knuckle boxing matches. But once the English courts had stopped transporting convicts down-under, the tradition of bare-knuckle fights had slowly disappeared. As a result, even those young Aussies who did box regularly quickly discovered that being hit hard with bare knuckles hurt like shit and they didn't like taking too much of that sort of punishment in the ring.

Cracker found that even the tough-looking young Aussies quickly changed from attack to defence after he had given them a few good hard belts with his bare fists. As a result, Cracker didn't have too much difficulty in disposing of many a young Aussie in the course of an evening's entertainment, when he might have to face up to a score of wannabes in the ring. But it was good money and there weren't many fellas who succeeded in landing any really damaging punches.

For nearly two years, Cracker was happy going from town to town with the fair and Big Al as his manager. He had come to trust Big Al for his sound advice and no nonsense approach to the job in hand. Both men understood that, the more they built up Cracker as the greatest fighter in Australia the more money they would take from the punters who wanted to chance their arm. Cracker was happy to continue as long as he remained top dog.

Cracker enjoyed his life down-under. He had the lovely Mimi who lived with him, looked after him, cooked for him, washed his clothes and patched him up whenever he got hurt in the ring. He had not only become accepted by nearly everyone in the fair who lived together like an extended family but, understandably, with his growing reputation, the fair was going from strength to strength. Never had the fair attracted so many visitors, never had the takings been so high.

Then 'Clubber' arrived on the scene.

He was a giant of a man, some 6ft 6in tall, weighing 17 stone and not yet 30 years of age. He had arrived with his family from Central Europe, impoverished immigants speaking only Romanian and very little English. They had settled in Melbourne and started to work in the markets where many eastern and western Europeans, market gardeners and small farmers, lived.

But the young Romanian had grown restless and had set off to Sydney in search of a new life. He got a job as lifeguard and was persuaded to take up boxing. He was quite fast and very powerful. He also had a tremendous punch, a right cross, which, when it connected, usually flattened opponents outright.

Cracker sensed trouble as soon as the Romanian, nicknamed Clubber, entered the ring. Cracker could tell he was a trained boxer the moment he squared up to him at the opening bell. He looked the part. He also looked hungry and aggressive. Clubber was 9in taller than Cracker, 5 stone heavier and with a far longer reach. Cracker knew that his only chance of success was to hurt him, and quickly, because he guessed his opponent had probably never fought a bare-knuckle match in his life.

After a quiet, slow start, Cracker caught him with two hard punches to the head and followed up with four rapid punches to the body. The giant Romanian barely flinched but immediately came after Cracker. It was then that Cracker knew, for the first time in his life, that he had met his match and would find it very difficult to win this fight. But the crowds around the ring at Bendigo, numbering nearly 1,000 men, were screaming for the Romanian to knock down the scarfaced Pommie.

Suddenly, Cracker realised too late that he had walked into a real haymaker which hammered the left side of his head. Momentarily, he fell back on the ropes and shook his head. His left ear was hurting like hell and his head was thumping. Within 20 seconds, Clubber was knocking hell out of him again, this time smashing a left to the side of the head and hitting him directly on the ear again. Cracker managed to get some hard punches to Clubber's face and his nose started to bleed but he behaved as though he hadn't been touched. Two more smashes to the side of his head and Cracker knew his ear-drum had burst and blood was oozing out of his ear. Another three cracks and the other ear had punctured and the blood dribbled down his neck. It seemed the more blood the two men shed, the more the crowd loved what had become a fantastic fight.

The noise coming from the ring brought other members of the troupe to see what was going on and they didn't like what they saw. Their hero Cracker was being given a right going over and most of the blood seemed to be coming from him, though it was difficult to tell. For nearly 30 seconds, both men stood in the centre of the ring, toe to toe, trading punches to the head and the body. By the end of that encounter, Cracker knew he had little or no hope of stopping this big bastard. He changed tactics. He decided to stop trying to hit the fella but weave and bob instead, trying to lead him a dance around the ring which might help to exhaust him. If he could, Cracker believed he might have a chance of victory for he could then knock fuck out of the exhausted giant.

But it was not to be. Cracker tired before the giant, who simply plodded round the ring after him, throwing a punch whenever he got within range. Cracker looked across to Big Al for inspiration but he just shrugged his shoulders; he had no ideas either. He caught a glimpse of Mimi, too, but he could tell from the look on her face that she was worried for him. So was Cracker.

For 15 long minutes the fight continued, but Cracker was getting tired of hitting the big man and even more tired of being thumped by the Romanian who seemed to have inexhaustable stamina. Cracker could see his $100 challenge purse being lost. That renewed his vigour and he steeled himself for one final, devastating attack. For 30 seconds he threw everything he had in his locker at Clubber, splitting his mouth open, pulverising his shattered, bloody nose, but all to no avail. Clubber kept returning and landing haymakers that hurt. Cracker walked into a shuddering right and felt his knees give way. Before he hit the canvas, two more crashing blows had landed either side of his head.

He came round to hear the crowds cheering and through swollen, battered eyes, he could just see the Romanian giant walking round the ring punching the air in celebration as the spectators cheered and cheered. Cracker heard Big Al telling him to stay still, then helping him out of the ring to the sound of cheers and boos. He didn't know whether the boos were for him or not and he didn't care. Never in his life had Cracker taken such a beating. He was taken to a trailer where he sat on the bed while Mimi washed away the blood that covered his face, neck and torso.

The next morning, Cracker woke, still suffering from pain in both ears. His battered pulp of a face felt

OK, though he had a thumping headache, the like of which he had never known before. When he looked in the mirror, he had the shock of his life. His nose was split open and looked as though it had been hit with bricks; his eyes were still half-closed, puffy and various colours of yellow, black and blue. His whole face was a mass of dried blood, and when he felt it, the bruising still hurt. When he took a deep breath, he could feel his ribs hurting and wondered if they were broken or cracked. He felt a real mess.

But that mattered little to Cracker. Far more importantly, his pride had taken a battering and so had his confidence. For two years he had been the king of the bare-knuckle world in Australia and now, in one night, it had all gone. What really hurt was the thought that he felt in his heart that he could never gain a victory against the Romanian giant. He was simply too big, too hard, too strong and too fast. He also threw a crushing right cross.

Cracker told Big Al that he had to get away. He had been fighting virtually non-stop for more than two years and needed a break. He also needed to restore his own confidence and to sort out his body which had taken an almighty beating that night. Cracker also knew that when word got around that Scarface Pommie had been soundly beaten in the ring, every young buck and his dog would be high-tailing it to the fair to have a crack at him. He didn't fancy that.

Accompanied by Mimi, he took off for Sydney. They took a room in a small hotel in King's Cross and Cracker took Mimi to all his old haunts. He went to look for his three girls but they had disappeared and no one knew where they had gone or where they now lived. He took Mimi to his sea-front pub at Bondi but the manager had left to go to Perth in Western Australia. He knew no one.

Cracker showed Mimi all his old haunts and they spent time in the bars and on the beaches, sunbathing and swimming. Cracker was really enjoying himself. It was the first holiday he had ever taken in his life. For the first time since he had arrived in Australia, a penniless stranger without a job, Cracker relaxed. His young body recovered rapidly and he began to feel good again. He discovered he liked doing nothing and he found he enjoyed his booze. The summer days melted into autumn and still Cracker and Mimi lived together in the poky hotel room. Now they were spending more time in pubs and clubs and Cracker put on weight and woke in the morning with hangovers. By his side, the faithful Mimi never complained; she worshipped him.

But when the rains came and the clouds gathered over Sydney harbour, Cracker suddenly had a powerful desire to return home to his folks. He hadn't spoken to them since leaving Britain and he had never written because he didn't know where they might be living or what he would say. He wondered about the police but thought that his little misdemeanour would be long forgotten; he didn't believe in the long arm of the law.

Mimi guessed what was going on in his mind and guessed he would not take her back to Britain with him. One morning, she went out to buy some milk and bread for toast and never returned. But as he was packing his bag before flying back to Britain, Cracker found a note. It read simply, 'Good luck, Cracker. Thanks for everything. I shall love you always. Mimi.'

CHAPTER 10

Many tough, hard bastards, who know and respect those street warriors who have ruled the bare-knuckle world for some years, understand there is often a fine line between their love of hard-fought fights and out-right, naked violence.

Some street warriors treat bare-knuckle, no-holds-barred fighting as a way of life, but others find it difficult, if not impossible, to control their emotions and their violence when the fights turn nasty. During the course of a fight, some hard men seem to turn from rough, tough fighters to berserk maniacs, hell-bent on destroying their opponents as savagely and brutally as possible.

One such street-warrior was Mick 'the Madman' McShea who became a legend before he was 40 years old. Born into a large Irish family in the 1950s, Mick grew up to become a tousle-haired teenager who spent his time in the school playground persuading other boys to fight. As a result, he earned himself a nickname – Basher – that he was never to lose. Invariably, Basher won all his schoolboy fights and caused great mayhem among his pals and enemies alike. He just loved fighting, anyone, any time. Always in trouble, always fighting, his mother packed him off to the British Army at the age of 17.

She told him, 'The Army's for fighting and you want to do nothing else but fight so you had better go and earn a living at the same time.'

Basher accepted his mother's advice, took the ferry to Scotland and joined the Black Watch. He became a good soldier but, at the same time, he also became a good boxer. An army physical training instructor, a sergeant everyone called Mac, took Basher under his wing after he saw him beat up another soldier in a barrack room brawl.

Despite having no training, Basher had a ferocity, a violence about his approach to boxing which the PTI hoped he could channel into a constructive boxing technique in the ring when he would be wearing gloves and fighting according to the Queensberry Rules. After finishing his basic training with the regiment, the PTI found Basher a cushy job in the stores and began the task of turning his young protégé from a wild, violent fighter into a professional, world-class boxer.

But it would be an uphill struggle.

Basher was put through a tough training schedule. The PTI would have the teenager running five miles before breakfast and then would take him to the regimental gym for weights, punch-bag boxing and teaching him the basic skills of attack and defence. After lunch, Basher would do two hours of circuit training and then be sent to the stores to finish off his day's official work.

When Basher was allowed out of camp with his mates, however, the trouble would begin. No matter if Basher and his army pals only went to the cinema, the evening would probably end in a punch-up with some local lads who enjoyed taking the piss out of the young army recruits. Quickly, Basher would take offence and, in no time, he would be amongst the local lads knocking shit out of them.

Basher also took a pride in being a soldier in the Black Watch, one of Scotland's proudest regiments with a magnificent history of bravery and valour in battles and wars across the world. Anyone who dared to shit on the Black Watch in the presence of Basher McShea had to face his wrath and his fists. Basher didn't ask questions in such situations; he simply waded in with his fists flying. He would never retreat, even in the face of a mob of lads throwing punches at him, but would stand and take whatever they threw at him – and then smash the fuck out of the bastards.

One night in Glasgow, Basher had enjoyed a few drinks with his soldier mates when trouble brewed with a gang of local lads who took the piss out of Basher because of his Irish accent. At first, he took no notice and Basher and his pals moved on to another pub. As they were leaving that pub some time after 11.00pm, the gang of Scottish lads were waiting for them.

Basher recalled what happened. 'Most of my mates had already left the pub and I walked out with two of my pals some time later. As soon as we walked into the street, a gang of six lads came towards us challenging us to a fight. We didn't want to know. It had been a great night out and we just wanted to get back to barracks. We moved out into the road to walk past them but they squared up in front of us, blocking our way. Then the jeering started, calling me fucking names for being Irish and joining a Scottish regiment. We tried to walk on, but they stood their ground challenging us with their fists, daring us to throw the first punch.

'We tried to walk on but they wouldn't move. I realised they were pissed but we had also had a few.

'I was getting annoyed with these lads and I knew there was a real chance that I would lose my cool, totally lose it. I could feel the tension, the violence mounting inside me. I told my two mates to follow me and I just went to walk around them. One asked me what the fuck I thought I was doing, and then he hit me.

'That was it. I just saw red. I smashed him with a clubbing right and a vicious left which knocked his head right back. His eyes looked up to the sky and he fell backwards. Another lad threw a punch but missed and I turned and gave him two horrendous smacks in the face with my fists clenched. I could tell I had done real damage to the little bastard 'cos he just turned away, his hands covering his face. My two mates were dealing with two more of them but I couldn't tell if they were winning or losing. It seemed a bit of a grappling mess. Two others tried to jump me, so I grabbed one by the collar and his trousers and smashed his head into a wall. He let out a scream so I smashed his head once more into the wall and dropped him. His mate had jumped on my back so I put my arm around his neck and smashed my other fist into his face. He couldn't escape. I must have smashed him half-a-dozen times in the face and I saw the claret spill as his nose split open. Then I let him go, throwing him to the ground and put in the boot as he fell to the ground. I aimed for his face and his guts, kicking him as hard as I fucking could. These bastards had annoyed me and I was giving them fuck. They had asked for it.

'Three or four of their lads were starting to get to their feet so I shouted to my mates that it was time to fuck off and we walked away. No one followed us.'

Basher McShea's reputation was enhanced by that ruckus and he earned respect from his mates in the regiment. As a result, his mates enjoyed going out with Basher for a Friday night piss-up, happy to buy him booze, in the knowledge that if trouble did develop he would be on hand to sort out the shit with his fists.

After three months of sparring and getting really fit, his PTI sergeant decided to put Basher into the ring for a regimental contest. It was no contest. Within 20 seconds, Basher had his opponent out cold. At the opening bell, Basher had run across the ring and began throwing punches at the unfortunate boxer who simply had no defence against the barrage Basher unleashed. Basher's opponent was a competent boxer but he had no way of escaping Basher's punches.

Within six months, Basher, who had developed into a light-heavyweight, was fighting inter-regimental boxing matches against stiff opposition and he won virtually every fight inside the distance. There was only one trouble. If his opponent really hurt Basher, out-punched or out-boxed him, Basher was unable to control his temper and he would then forget everything he had been taught and stand in front of his opponent while the two men slugged it out, toe to toe. On those occasions, Basher invariably won because the ferocity of his punching destroyed his opponent even if Basher did take a load of punishment himself.

The end of Basher's boxing career in the Army came after he had served 18 months with the Black Watch. He had been entered in a boxing match against a well-built heavyweight, an army sergeant in his late twenties, who had had a formidable career, representing the army boxing team on a number of occasions. Basher was happy to accept the challenge despite the weight disadvantage.

The contest, held in Glasgow, was a sell-out and the hall was packed to the rafters. Mick McShea's reputation had earned him a great following, not only in the Black Watch, but throughout Glasgow's boxing fans. People were always keen to watch Basher fight because he could be so ferocious. He never went into the ring and danced around, throwing the odd punch at his opponent. Basher wanted to use his fists from the very first bell and that made for some of the best boxing ever seen in Glasgow. There had been other men keen to fight from the first bell but most had lacked the ferocity of Basher. The fact that he never retreated, never flinched in the punch but would relentlessly move forward, his fists flying, until he had smashed his opponent to the canvas, won him great praise and a dedicated following.

But this Sergeant was good. In the first two rounds he defended himself superbly and threw counter-punches which troubled Basher, hitting him in the face or the pit of the stomach with relentless repetition. In the third round, Basher threw caution to the wind and began to trade punches toe to toe with the beefy Sergeant. But the Sergeant was stronger and heavier and every time he landed a good punch on Basher, he tormented him, baiting him to punch harder.

Basher was coming off worse in this fight and he knew it. The Sergeant knew it as well and that was why he danced around, teased and ridiculed him in an effort to tempt Basher to explode. The Sergeant had heard of Basher's violence which made him fight like a madman, throwing caution to the wind. He had heard of the number of boxers who had been destroyed by Basher's violence in the ring and he wanted to teach the young Irish upstart a lesson he would never forget.

Suddenly, dramatically, the fight changed. Basher got to his feet for the fourth and ran like a stag at the Sergeant, catching him unawares. The crowd roared their approval for this was the Basher they had come to see. They wanted blood and they sensed they were about to see it. The question on everyone's mind was: whose blood?

Three savage punches later and the Sergeant was reeling. The crowd roared as they saw claret oozing from a cut over his eye. But this Sergeant, this champion, was no pushover. He defended himself with lefts, keeping Basher at bay until his head cleared and he could think straight again.

Basher stepped up the fight again, running towards his opponent and catching him with a right and a left, then another one-two, to the side of the head. He had hurt the Sergeant who, for the first time, began to retreat. Basher moved in for the kill but suddenly the Sergeant appeared to stumble and smashed his head into Basher's face with a tremendous crack. Basher's nose split open and he fell back concussed. Basher was convinced that had been no accidental clash of heads because it had been so ferocious. He knew it had been deliberate. In that instant, Basher saw red.

Now he was determined to smash the Sergeant, to hurt him physically, maim him if possible because, when he was about to be beaten, he had played dirty. Basher took no notice of the punches that were hitting his face and body as he stood in front of the Sergeant crashing punch after punch into his face, aiming for the cut over his eye. Basher wanted to shut that eye completely so he could concentrate on closing the other. In that instant, he wanted to blind the bastard and then cut loose, smashing his face to a pulp. He wanted to teach him a lesson he would never forget.

The Sergeant's eye closed after four hard punches and he looked in desperation at Basher. Basher smiled to himself, knowing the job was half-done. He then went like a tiger for the other eye, crashing punches into his face. The Sergeant was moving backwards desperately trying to defend himself from the onslaught. But Basher hadn't finished. He didn't stop for one second; never gave him a breather but crashed punch after punch into him; left, right, left, right.

The crowd were roaring as the blood flowed down the Sergeant's face, arms and body. The sight of his opponent's blood seemed to give Basher a new lease of life. He trapped the Sergeant in a corner and began belting him, one punch landing every second. The Sergeant's corner threw in the towel but Basher didn't want to know. He crashed more punches into the man's face and his other eye closed. The referee came forwards to stop the fight but Basher continued. As the Sergeant crumpled to the floor, Basher followed him down with a crescendo of violent punches. And as the Sergeant's limp body hit the canvas, Basher went in with the boot, aiming at the man's head and face and kicking with ferocious violence. With every kick, the man's head was jerked backwards. The Sergeant's corner jumped into the ring, and with the help of the referee, four men managed to haul Basher away. Only then did Basher hear the extraordinary roars of the crowd.

But the fight wasn't over yet. Not for Basher. Within seconds, the ring filled with ten or more angry, beefy spectators who dashed over to Basher their fists flying. They were angry that someone, anyone, could treat their boxing hero like that and they wanted to have a go at Basher and teach him a lesson. After five or six hard bare-knuckle punches to the face and body, Basher erupted again. He swung his fists at anyone who came into range.

At one time, Basher was on the ropes with eight or nine men surrounding him, all trying to smash him. But every time one bare fist landed on Basher's face, he lashed out. Before long, three men were lying around his feet and Basher alternated between kicking the fuck out of those on the floor and belting in the face those still standing. The referee, officials and army personnel leapt into the ring in an effort to stop the mayhem which the crowd were loving and cheering. They had never in their lives seen a fight end like this; never before seen a boxer taking on ten men determined to knock shit out of him at the end of a fight.

For five minutes, the chaos continued. The entire stadium had erupted and the noise was deafening. No one in the ring could hear what was being shouted and no one cared. Basher was in his element and the red mist descended once more. He moved forward, taking out one man at a time, hitting everyone as hard as he could. None of them had any defence; they only knew how to throw punches but none could get in a real swing, a hard punch. Basher grabbed two men and cracked their heads together with such force they collapsed on the canvas in front of him. Suddenly, the others backed off. They had seen enough and taken enough punishment.

Basher's corner got in between Basher and those men still standing, forming a protective ring around their champion boxer and the red mist disappeared. Basher sat down on his corner seat and let his men take off his gloves.

Now everyone who witnessed that extraordinary fight knew that Mick McShea was a 'madman' and his reputation for violence became enshrined in the annals of the Black Watch. But he had gone too far. Unable to control his violent temper, Basher knew his future was in doubt. Though Basher had won a famous victory, it would be the last time he ever fought in the Army. Because of his refusal to end the fight and, instead, had weighed in with the boot, almost blinding the Sergeant, the decision was taken that he should end his army career and be discharged from the Black Watch.

Basher was unhappy with the decision but there was nothing he could do. He realised perfectly well that in certain circumstances he simply could not control his temper and that, when he did lose his cool, he would go berserk, not feeling any injury or any wound, but became totally galvanised to hurt, injure, destroy and even kill an opponent.

Out of the Army, out of work and needing to earn a living, Mick McShea searched in vain for a job. By chance, Basher met a girl whose father ran a pub in Manchester, a pub where bare-knuckle fights took place in the vast space in the roof of the building which he had converted into a secret boxing den. There was a roped ring and room for 200 spectators.

He had been dating his new girl Sharon for a month before she mentioned that her father organised bare-knuckle fights. Sharon knew all about bare-knuckle fighting and she understood the passion which some men held for the sport. She had heard her father and the regulars talking so often about the fight game, as a good, old-fashioned and honest sport and she had seen one or two fights herself.

Sharon's father Ronnie was very interested to hear details of Basher's boxing career, especially as he had fought in army contests. But he was worried that Basher was simply a good amateur boxer and would be unable to adapt to the vicious life of bare-knuckle fighting which was so much more wild and wounding than even the professional ring. He arranged for Basher to attend a local boxing gym where he fixed up a couple of rounds with a sparring partner under his expert eye.

The owner of the gymnasium, who had himself been a bare-knuckle fighter, chatted to Ronnie while the sparring was going on. 'Can't tell really,' he said, 'I'll need to see him in a short, real fight first. I'll arrange it.'

Seven days later, Basher McShea went to witness a bare-knuckle fight in Ronnie's private gym above the pub. It was the first such fight he had ever seen. And he was most impressed.

He said later, 'I was captivated from the very first punch. This was real boxing, real fighting. This was what I had dreamed boxing was all about in the good old days before boxers wore gloves and before the Queensberry Rules came into force. I felt every single punch that landed and felt the pain when a bone-crusher hit home. But I felt my adrenalin flowing at the very thought of stepping into the ring with a bare-knuckle fighter. I smiled when I saw the winner kick fuck out of the poor bastard on the floor because that was the very reason I had been kicked out of the Army.'

That night, Basher sought out Ronnie and asked him to organise a trial fight for him. 'Anywhere, any time,' he said.

Within two weeks, Basher had given his first real bare-knuckle fight as Ronnie's protégé after passing his trial fight with flying colours. He had, in fact, destroyed his opponent inside three minutes and not shown a sign of the madcap violence he was prone to. Sharon came along to watch.

Basher was put up against a middleweight gypsy boy who had been in the ring for five years. He looked rough and tough and his corner and half the gym was filled with his relatives and friends.

Basher would later recall that first bare-knuckle bout. 'I was a bit apprehensive as they put on the bandages but the adrenalin was flowing. I kept looking over at my oppo wondering how tough he was and what sort of fighter he really was. I didn't really know what to expect but Ronnie had told me to concentrate on attack and forget defence.

'At the bell, this lad who must have been about my age, came racing out like a fucking bull but I chopped him on the side of the neck before he could hit me. He went past my left side and into the ropes before turning round. As he turned, I hit him hard and low, making him double up. Then, as his head came forward, I let him have a hard uppercut with my left, knocking his head back 'til it seemed his neck would break.

'I backed off like you do when boxing, which might have been a mistake. It gave my oppo a chance to clear his head and come charging at me again, his arms swinging like fucking flappers. He caught me with a left and a right to the head but I didn't move back and held my position, and counter-attacked with half-a-dozen shots to the body and the head. He didn't seem to like that.

'The fight went fairly evenly for about six minutes with the crowds cheering both of us. It seemed that everyone who wasn't a gyppo yelled for me. I liked that, it gave me confidence. He was a tough bugger but I was determined to give him a proper pasting when he started to slow down. But he didn't slow.'

In fact, the gyppo got the upper hand, then Basher slipped on some blood and fell to the canvas. In a split-second, the gypsy boy was into him, his fists cracking his head, his feet kicking fuck out of Basher's body. At one stage he jumped on Basher, knocking the wind out of him. It was that final act of vandalism that enraged Basher.

He said later, 'I got to my feet and fought for my breath before the bastard came back at me. He must have thought he had all but won the fight. But as I saw him half-smiling, my adrenalin worked overtime and I just saw that grinning fucking face. That was it. I tore at him. He tried to hit back but I didn't even notice his punches though some must have landed. I just kept smashing my fists into his face and suddenly he was going backwards and I was following him around the ring, punching, punching, punching at that fucking face with the half-smile. He had tried to end the fight by jumping on my kidneys and my lungs but now I was determined to finish the fight by knocking his silly face to pulp. I went wild, berserk. I wanted to destroy him, to maim him for life.'

As the gypsy fell slowly to the canvas, trying to hold on to the ropes, Basher continued thumping him, smashing his abdomen, then his rib cage and finally his bloodied face. As he hit the floor, Basher began to boot him in the ribs and in the face. He wouldn't stop even though the man was lying unconscious on the floor.

He said later, 'The next thing I knew I was grabbed from behind and dragged away from the lad. I could hear the cheers around the gym and I could see the lad lying face down with blood surrounding his head. He looked unconscious, totally out of it, and I was glad.'

'Fucking fantastic ... fucking fantastic,' were Ronnie's shouted words of praise as he held Mick's hand above his head in a victory salute to the crowd.

That night, Ronnie handed Mick £500 in notes and told him there would be plenty more if he wanted to continue in the bare-knuckle game.

'You're on,' Mick replied, 'lay on whoever you want and I'll deal with him.'

Mick went back to the flat he shared with Sharon feeling on top of the world. He confessed later, 'Sharon and I had a couple of drinks before heading home. That night was incredible. I just wanted to fuck and fuck and fuck. I didn't feel tired, I didn't want to sleep. We must have done it half-a-dozen times or more before we went to sleep.

'Every time I fought, I felt the same way afterwards and Sharon loved it. We would usually fuck for four or five hours non-stop. I suppose it was the adrenalin I had built up during the fight. If my face had received a real pasting during the fight we would fuck with the light out so she didn't have to see my bloodied, bruised and battered face. If it was OK, we kept the light on.'

Basher McShea toured Britain with Sharon, taking part in bare-knuckle fights that had been arranged by her father. Sometimes he was present, at other times he would stay at home. But, although Mick lost the odd fight, and sometimes took a belting, for more than two years he fought anyone who was put up against him. Mick wasn't into trophies or titles; he just wanted the glory of winning and a big fat wad of notes afterwards.

Then tragedy struck.

Mick and Sharon were driving home to Manchester after a fight in East London when their car – a new car Mick had bought with his winnings – was involved in a multiple pile-up on the M6. Sharon was killed and Mick's legs were smashed to pulp. He had fought his last fight.

Another hard bastard who could be highly dangerous when roused to action was Reggie Parker, a legendary figure who had a reputation for being one of the most ruthless security men the club scene has ever known.

Many club owners throughout London had cause to know Reggie Parker well, very well. He was responsible for saving a dozen or more clubs from going under because he was called in to sort out security problems. The great majority of club owners had called in Reg to take on the hard men, the gypsies and other hard gangs, who terrorised decent, law-abiding clubbers and their owners. These gangs, usually six or eight strong, would walk into a club, drink all night and then leave without paying.

These gangs would often scare the shit out of the waitresses, threatening to cut them up or knock fuck out of them unless they brought them food and drinks 'at the double'. These men sometimes treated the girls like their slaves, as if they owned their bodies. They would touch them, stroke their thighs and bottoms, pinch their tits. If the waitresses dared say 'no' or threaten to complain to their boss, the gang members would warn them they would be 'cut up' or 'done over' outside. No girls wanted to risk that and so they, too, would quit the job.

When the club owner fronted them, demanding they pay the bill, there would be immediate trouble. Sometimes, these gangs would simply trash the club, breaking everything in sight, including glasses, bottles, mirrors, tables and chairs. They would scare the shit out of everyone in that club in their vicious violence. Then they would walk out. But they wouldn't pay.

Sometimes, these gangs would wait 'til the end of the night's drinking and then wait outside for the owner to lock up. On occasions, club owners were lucky to escape with their lives. They would often be beaten to a pulp and left unconscious by the side of the road as a warning to other club owners.

During the evening, if any clubbers complained of the gang's loud, sometimes violent behaviour, the club members would be warned to shut up or risk a beating. Of course, nearly every clubber just shut up or walked out of the club never to return.

Club owners would be in despair as they saw their trade disappearing out of the door as the bully-boys terrorised their clubs and intimidated the staff and the clubbers. Often, a club owner had invested all his savings, and sometimes mortgaged his home, to set up a good, respectable club and he would be at his wits' end, not knowing how to deal with the never-ending problem.

Some contemplated going to the police for protection but shelved the idea quickly. Other club owners had warned them that if that happened, the gang would simply trash the place as punishment and disappear never to be traced. It was a no-win situation.

NICHOLAS DAVIES / 224

That's where Reggie Parker proved such a diamond.

Of course, there were many hard men who formed unofficial security teams to guard clubs. The Krays used to do it very professionally. But their method was equally as vicious as the gangs who terrorised the clubs. The Kray brothers practised the age-old, well-known 'protection racket' offering to 'protect' clubs with their men. If the club owner refused, for whatever reason, the Krays would send in their security men to smash the place to pieces for refusing their offer. After one or two such visits, the poor club owner would then gladly accept the Kray brothers' offer.

Reggie Parker and many other security teams who focused on clubs didn't work like that. These men were simply paid for looking after a club and dealing with gangs who tried to ruin a night out for clubbers, bully their way to eating and drinking for free or terrorise staff and owners.

The strong, powerfully-built Parker would usually receive a message from a desperate club owner pleading for assistance. Parker would go along and have a chat with the owner, checking the level of violence and trouble that was ruining the man's business. Most stories were the same.

For weeks, if not months, a gang of local thugs – sometimes gypsies, at other times a group of violent young men – would arrive at the club in question and barge their way in without paying a penny. On many occasions, these gangs of bullies would arrive armed with chains, machetes, iron bars, hammers, blades and open razors and, occasionally, even guns. They would walk to the bar and order drinks and, quite often, they would order whatever was on the menu, demanding they be treated like honoured guests. If they fancied the look of a girl who was also visiting the club, they would try to pull her, even if she was on a date. If the boyfriend protested, members of the gang would intervene and threaten the man with a 'belting' if he didn't shut up and sit down. If he did try to intervene, he would, more often than not, be beaten up.

On occasions, they would go and beat up some innocent stranger who was quietly having a drink on his own, simply because they didn't like the way he looked or dressed. They would usually start by being rude or making offensive remarks and when the stranger dared to reply, they would take that as an excuse for a fight. But the fights of the bully-boys would never be one-on-one but usually four or five against one poor bastard.

These gangs thought they were untouchable. They believed they could walk into any nightclub, drink and eat whatever they wanted and then walk out without paying. They knew the owners would never call the law because they would always be the loser. When the police had disappeared, the gang would return another night and smash the place to bits!

Reggie Parker would usually agree to look after the security of the club on two conditions. One, he wanted to be paid; and two, he demanded that he employ his own men on the door. The sensible owners were happy to go along with that deal.

Reg Parker told what happened at one club he had agreed to take care of. 'On the Thursday night, I assembled five of my most trusted men and I made sure all were armed – not with guns, but just weapons in case real trouble broke out. Within easy reach was my baseball bat. Clubbers started to arrive at around 11.00pm as usual and all were treated with civility.

'Some time around midnight, a taxi pulled up outside and three men got out. They were well pissed and laughing loudly. Reg recognised them as gypsies because of their boots and gold sovereign rings. As they attempted to walk in, I politely told them they weren't allowed to enter. For 30 seconds their leader, a big, well-built bastard in his late thirties, eye-balled me and then turned and left. I guessed he was going for reinforcements.

'Within 30 minutes, a beaten-up white Ford Transit van pulled up outside the club and a dozen men climbed out of the back. All were carrying iron bars and pieces of hard wood. I was about to become a very angry man.

'As the leader came towards me holding an iron bar, I rushed from the club and smashed the bastard over the head with my baseball bat. He dropped to his knees and blood trickled down his face. Another gypsy raised his iron bar and was about to bring it down on my head when I smashed him with my baseball bat.

'Within seconds, a row broke out and me and my lads, all armed with baseball bats, got stuck into the bastards. We cracked their heads as hard as we possibly could because we were determined to show them we were in charge.

'I kept shouting at them, "Fuck off ... I run this place now,' but they kept attacking us with their iron bars and clubs. I targeted the men with the iron bars because I knew they could cause real damage. At one stage, I became so enraged that I nearly lost it. If I had, I would have probably ended up killing one or two of them. I know that if I ever lose it, I am totally out of control, out of my mind with anger. On those occasions, all I want to do is destroy the bastard.

'After five minutes of smashing, thumping, cursing and injuries, the men retreated, shouting that they would be back. I told them to fuck off and never return. I knew they would be back.'

Reggie Parker knew the bully-boys well. He was right. They came back every few nights, sometimes armed, sometimes drunk and sometimes hell bent on a fight. At other times, they tried to sneak into the club pretending to be innocent clubbers. Reggie would have none of it. Whenever trouble arose, he dealt with it as harshly as he had that first night, breaking a few heads with his baseball bats and smashing a few bones. Eventually, his method of keeping order worked. After two months, the gang of gypsies were never to return. Reg and his team of security men continued their nightly duties for years. The club became peaceful and the owner prosperous.

There were many occasions in Reg Parker's life that he did lose it and those that saw it were in awe of the man. When in a rage, Reggie forgot everyone and everything except the man he was targeting. On those occasions, blind rage would take over his mind.

On one of a thousand such occasions in a London club, a drunk upset Reg because he refused to stop drinking, refused to sit down quietly and refused to go home. For 15 minutes Reg was his old, kind, gentle self, the man all his friends knew well. Then suddenly the stupid drunk, a strong, powerful man, got tough.

'If you're so fucking tough, throw me out,' the drunk shouted at Reggie.

Reggie didn't like that one bit. He leapt to his feet, walked briskly over to the drunk standing in the middle of the dance floor and smashed him full in the throat, causing the man to gasp for breath as if he was about to die. The drunk collapsed in a heap. But Reggie wasn't finished yet. He picked up the guy by the scruff of his jacket, dragged him along the floor like a rag doll and dumped him at the top of the stairs. Then Reg kicked him hard in the middle of the back, sending him hurtling to the bottom of the stairs, arms and legs flying everywhere.

Reg ran down the stairs and jumped on the man's head as he lay half-unconscious on the floor. Both Reg's feet landed on the man's head with a thumping, muffled crunch. It seemed to onlookers as though the man would never recover, but that horrendous attack still didn't satisfy Reg. He was in a mindless state of absolute fury. He seemed out of control; on the edge of madness. He wanted vengeance and he was determined to get it. As the man stirred, Reg took a step forward and then kicked the man as though he was taking a football penalty. Crack, the drunk's head spun away and he was out. He didn't move a muscle. Reg was just about to put in the boot once again but the other stewards jumped in, telling Reg, 'That's enough, mate ... that's enough.'

EPILOGUE

Bare-knuckle fighting in Britain is still very much alive and well in the twenty-first century, despite the fact that it is totally illegal and punishable by heavy fines. Those men who support or take part in this great traditional British sport – the toughest sporting contests in the world today – are continuing a proud national custom that has lasted for centuries.

Today, in secret bare-knuckle fights up and down the country, young men pit their skill, strength and courage against one another in the most basic contests of all. And they fight not just for money but for the honour and prestige such victories bring to their reputations and, in some instances, to their families.

Today's fights are just as tough, fearsome and vicious as they always have been with the fighters giving no quarter and asking no favours. Today, the fights only end when one man is unable to continue, often unable to stand and sometimes barely conscious.

On most occasions, the fighters still inflict the most gruesome, horrific and dreadful damage to each other, particularly around the face. At the end of most fights, noses have been split open, eyes gouged, mouths ripped open, teeth broken and cheeks bruised, damaged and split. Blood is everywhere. The fighters, always stripped to the waist, are literally covered in blood from their various wounds.

And it is not only the defeated man who is wounded, sometimes for life. One of the less well-known side-effects of highly successful bare-knuckle champions is the fact that their hands become so badly bruised and damaged that gangrene sets in, which, in some cases, eventually causes death. But that usually affects only those who practise the art of bare-knuckle fighting over many decades.

But there are some fighters who happily disprove the doctors and medics who warn of the dangers of bare-knuckle boxing. One such champion is Tucker Dunn from Appleby in Oxfordshire, who is still bare-knuckle fighting today at the age of 78!

'I have been fighting since my teens – in the 1930s – and I still happily accept challenges from anyone who dares to fight me. Without a doubt, bare-knuckle fighting is one of the world's true, honest sports where there is no hiding place for the weak, the coward or the bully. I love the sport because it attracts the bravest, most courageous men with guts and determination.'

There was the famous Welsh champion, Edwin

Thomas, who started bare-knuckle fighting in 1928 and continued fighting on a monthly basis until he retired at the age of 49. Edwin Thomas lived in the Welsh valleys and most of his bare-knuckle contests took place in the mountains around Merthyr Tydfil. His most famous fight lasted 2 hours 49 minutes and, on some occasions, he would fight two men at a time – and he usually won. But not always. He was one of the great champions who eventually died from gangrene.

There are a number of bare-knuckle fighters who take up the sport because their fathers, and their fathers before them, had been fighters, sometimes going back many generations. These men sometimes don't even know their grandparents had been bare-knuckle fighters and yet they find themselves inextricably drawn to the sport.

One such man is Brian Miller who, as a teenager, discovered that the sport of bare-knuckle fighting was somehow very appealing. He felt the urge to scrap, to fight in public, to take part in the sport and yet he had no idea whatsoever that, in earlier days, his relatives had been great bare-knuckle fighters, champions in fact.

Brian was attending a family funeral following the death of his uncle Johnny Miller and discovered that his uncle had been partly responsible for putting North Shields on the map back in the 1940s and 1950s due primarily to his achievements in the ring. One of Johnny Miller's great claims to fame was fighting and drawing against the great French European Champion Guy Grazier. The fight was so dramatic and exciting that, at the finish, spectators threw loads of money into the ring in appreciation.

Brian then discovered through research that one of his great-uncles, a man named Donald, had, in fact, been the Bare-Knuckle Champion of Sunderland in the 1930s.

But the great majority of bare-knuckle fighters are convinced that their sport is far less dangerous than the licensed contests in which boxing with gloves under the British Boxing Board of Control rules is the law.

Today, licensed boxers with heavily padded gloves can punch hell out of each other, ferociously thumping each other around the head as violently as possible. Understandably, such repeated battering of the head sometimes leads to damage, or even serious damage, to the boxer's brain. In bare-knuckle fighting such brain injuries are rare because there are far fewer 'heavy' punches to the head and, consequently, far less damage to the brain.

Throughout the past century, there have been numerous calls for a total ban on boxing because of the risks of brain damage faced by every boxer whenever he steps into the ring. The current furore over the dangers of boxing began in 1991 when Michael Watson was knocked unconscious after a bruising fight against Chris Eubank. Watson collapsed in the twelfth round and suffered serious brain damage. Today, he is partially paralysed.

Since 1986, three British professional boxers – Steve Watt, a welterweight; Bradley Stone, a superbantamweight; and Jimmy Murray, another bantamweight – have died as a result of injuries during boxing matches and several others have been seriously disabled. Statistically, however, boxing tragedies are rare.

Every year in Britain, there are about 200 professional boxing shows in which there are anything from three to fifteen contests. In total, therefore, there are something like 1,500 professional fights under Boxing Board of Control regulations every year. And those numbers do not include amateur fights in which contestants have to wear headguards as they do, for example, in the modern Olympic games.

The odds of something serious happening to a boxer are estimated to be about 3,000 to 1, and the great majority of boxers believe that the sport is safe despite the high-profile injuries which do occur from time to time. But what is accepted by the medical profession is that repeated punches to the head with gloved fists must ultimately damage the brain.

In December 2000, Paul Ingle, 28, collapsed at the end of a gruelling professional fight when defending his International Boxing Federation featherweight title against Mbulelo Botile in Sheffield. A scan revealed a blood clot on the brain caused by his opponent's punches. And these were only featherweight boxers.

By contrast, in bare-knuckle fighting there may be far more blood spilt than during professional and amateur fights; and far more broken noses, broken teeth, smashed jaws and broken ribs. But no one in the sport can remember a bare-knuckle fighter dying as a result of a fight.

Supporters of bare knuckles believe the sport is growing and will continue to grow for various reasons, despite active steps that are taken by the law to put a stop to the sport.

Gambling plays a major role in bare-knuckle fighting, with bets being laid throughout a fight as the two men's fortunes ebb and flow. Most bets are placed by enthusiastic punters before a fight takes place but unofficial bookmakers continue to take bets right up until the end of a fight, the odds changing rapidly as every serious wound takes its toll.

Nowadays, punters at most bare-knuckle affairs are more numerous than the enthusiasts who gather purely to watch two men knocking hell out of each other. Depending, of course, on the quality and fame of the fighters and the number of contests, the amount of money that exchanges hands can exceed tens of thousands of pounds. However, there are some men who drive hundreds of miles to watch a few bare-knuckle contests just to see the amount of blood that flows and the number of wounds inflicted. Some people say those supporters are the real enthusiasts.

For decades, those responsible for keeping the sport afloat came from Irish tinkers and gypsy families whose forefathers had always enjoyed a bit of bare-knuckle fighting. Many such families handed down the tradition from father to son and some families became famous simply because of the prowess of their young bare-knuckle fighters who literally fought, not for the money, but for the reputation and honour of their family.

And there are people who have great admiration for bare-knuckle fighters, men prepared to slug it out toe to toe, who have the courage and guts to take cutting punches and horrendous wounds and yet never give in until they are unable to stand. Bare-knuckle fighters, of course, show far greater bravery and often, take far worse punishment than any boxer who steps into the professional or amateur ring.

As a result, admiration for these heroes is growing apace. Many younger men, though few women, want to see something that is different, they want to indulge their senses in a sport that is all about blood and guts, strength and courage. In this day and age, when people are pampered and spend their spare time sitting in front of television sets, there are many young men aching to experience something different, more wild, adventurous, daring and courageous. Bare-knuckle fighting provides all this in spades.

And bare-knuckle fighting attracts those young people of this new century who crave anti-heroes, for the sport is often led by men of violence who channel that strength and courage into violent behaviour in which they can indulge themselves in a bare-knuckle fight. Every Friday and Saturday night the streets of Britain's town centres are alive with young men aching for a fight, a spot of violence, a dare-devil escapade that requires courage and in-your-face action.

And there is the very fact that bare-knuckle fights are against the law, against received wisdom, against the advice of the so-called Establishment who look down on bare-knuckle fighters as though they are beyond hope, people who should be stopped from participating in the sport at all costs. Those do-gooders say the sport is dangerous, cruel, barbaric, blood-thirsty and violent and must be stopped at all costs.

There are tens of thousands of young people, including women, who deliberately violate the law, who want to swim against the stream, who want to live a more dangerous life which they find interesting, daring and different and, more importantly, risky. They enjoy danger and the thought of danger in all its glory. They revel in it. And bare-knuckle provides that in spades!

And now there is the Internet.

The explosion of the Internet has included a dramatic increase in websites dedicated to bare-knuckle fighting and boxing as well as growing numbers of people making hits on the sites because of the rapidly escalating interest in this banned sport.

Over the past three years, American interest in the sport has taken off. Across America, the tough, hard men from Brooklyn to Texas to California, many of them from middle America, have taken a keen interest in learning about this sport which, in most respects, is new to American men. Of course, bare-knuckle fights were staged in the days of early America, and Westerns from the 1930s to the 1960s usually contained bare-knuckle fights, often wonderful, stunt-filled bar-room brawls in which scores of men would sometimes take part.

But those fights have died a death and there has been no bare-knuckle fighting of note in America since those days. Most tough, hard Americans who want to enjoy such physical sport have been channelled into amateur or professional boxing with gloves.

Brian Miller, 37, is one man who spreads the word across the globe on the Internet through *www.brianmiller.freeserve.co.uk,* his own dedicated website. He has recorded a growing interest in Americans wanting to know every detail of the sport and he is happily providing them with information. Reports are starting to come in from the USA telling of contests that are being set up in various states as more and more young men want to become involved.

Brian Miller, whose family have been involved in bare-knuckle fighting for generations, commented, 'This interest from America is exactly what the sport needs to give it a boost. If the Americans become actively involved, then it won't be long before fights are arranged over the Internet between fighters in America and the UK.

'I have already heard that Hollywood is interested in making a couple of movies using the fighters as anti-heroes. There seems to be a tremendous interest in the United States towards real hard men. The young men enjoy the sport and, I have been led to understand, the young women find the men who have the guts to take such punishment highly attractive.'

Some American women have revealed that they find such men highly attractive because they find the tremendous courage of the fighters a real turn-on. Martha Nelson from Texas, who enjoys watching wrestling on television and in the flesh, has written saying that tens of thousands of women every day watch strong men wrestling, in which no one gets hurt and no blood is spilled.

She commented, 'But women particularly are finding this wrestling has become tame. There are many women who would much prefer real bare-knuckle fights in which men throw punches, fighters get injured, blood is spilled and people don't get up and walk away but are often carried away unconscious, with blood and guts left behind on the ground.

'I can see American women taking to this because they want some reality in their lives. These women find the wrestlers sexually attractive but they tell me that they would find bare-knuckle fighters ten times more attractive because that sport needs raw courage. And women find themselves attracted to that; it's tough, it's hard and only real men have the guts to take part. Bare-knuckle fighting is new to modern America; it's dangerous, it's exciting and it's a real turn-on for many middle Americans. It has all the potential to really take off in the United States.'

Brian Miller, from North Shields, Tyne and Wear, has been able to trace family fighters back to 1863 when a great-great-grandfather named Robert Watson was born in Sunderland and began work as a blacksmith's striker in 1881. His father had died, so the teenage Robert had to earn enough money to feed the family. It seems that he managed to earn sufficient from bare-knuckle fighting, a sport in which he was both courageous and highly successful.

One side of Miller's family were Irish travellers, and the sons and grandsons of Robert Watson followed in his footsteps earning the family a well-deserved reputation as some of the foremost fighters in the north of England. Other Miller men enjoyed considerable success but there were some dark horses as well.

One relative, George Miller, another bare-knuckle fighter, had to flee the country after having a fight with a policeman in which the copper was soundly beaten. George ended up in Australia. Another relative, Francis Watson Helstern, was built for the sport and in the

1940s he was crowned King of Grimsby because of his outstanding bare-knuckle victories. Helstern, who feared no one and fought for the underdog, lost an eye during one horrendous fight but it still didn't stop him taking part in scores of other contests.

One of the most famous Miller family fighters was the great British middleweight boxing champion Randolph Turpin who, for many years, lived with Katie Miller. In 1950, Johnny Miller became a professional boxer and drew a fight with the European middleweight champion Guy Grazier, a Frenchman then considered one of the great boxers of his era.

Brian Miller commented, 'It's no wonder that me and other young men of the Miller family have found themselves attracted to the sport. We all love fighting. It seems to prove that fighters are indeed born, the genes passed down through the blood line. There must be many other young men around Britain today whose families have been involved in bare-knuckle fighting over generations who find themselves attracted to the sport but don't know why. If they traced their family tree, they, too, would probably find fighters going back through the generations.

'It's a sport like no other. It pumps the adrenalin; it produces heroes and villains; makes men of those who take part. The sport is also full of blood and guts and, above all, raw courage. And that is why the future of bare-knuckle fighting is bright, very bright.'

Other Titles from Blake Publishing

The Guv'nor
Lenny McLean

The number one best-selling book that began the hard man phenomenon. Lenny McLean was a man with many sides, known and feared, yet driven by an overwhelming desire to look after the welfare of his friends and family. His story is a tale of one man's triumphs against almost insurmountable odds, from a life of child abuse in East London to his tragic battle against cancer. This remarkable autobiography describes the extraordinary life of the man who has only ever needed to be called 'The Guv'nor'.
Hardback: £14.99

Pretty Boy
Roy Shaw

Violence for Roy 'Pretty Boy' Shaw is always business not pleasure, he's not a coward who can't do his own dirty work. He'd never hurt a woman, a child or the ordinary man in the street – he's not an unreasonable man. But as he says, 'if you are a man and you take a liberty with me or cross me, then believe me, when it comes to retribution I have no pity or conscience – if you're unlucky enough to have me come after you – beware – 'cos hell's coming with me ...'
Hardback: £14.99

Nosher
Nosher Powell

Nosher Powell is the ultimate hard man. Boxer, bouncer, minder, stunt man, he is truly a force to be reckoned with. As a heavyweight boxing champ he was equally at home in the world of unlicensed fighting as he was in the professional arena. He sparred with the legendary Muhammed Ali, as well as boxing greats Joe Louis and Sugar Ray Robinson. In seventy-eight professional fights Nosher was never once knocked out. 'The name of the game is respect. Lose it in my line of work, and you may as well emigrate!'
Paperback: £5.99

Bronson
Charles Bronson

Charles Bronson is Britain's most dangerous convict, with a reputation as the prison system's only serial hostage taker. His fearsome reputation has landed him in the toughest prison confinements in the country – dungeons, iron boxes concreted into the middle of cells and famously, in a cage like Hannibal Lecter. He has spent 22 of the last 26 years in solitary. Yet he is not a killer and has dealt with his gruelling life with humour – during a siege in 1993 he listed amongst his demands, an inflatable doll and a cup of tea.
Hardback: £14.99

Nigel Benn
Nigel Benn

Nigel Benn is a powerhouse amongst boxers. Known to his fans as the Dark Destroyer, his first 22 professional fights ended with him knocking out all his opponents – half of them before the first round was over. His incredible autobiography traces the course of his life from the grim days he spent in the army in Northern Island, to his notorious battle with Chris Eubank; from the numerous women he has romanced in the past, to the salvation he has found with his wife and adored children. From fighter to family man, this book explores the contrasts that make up the figure of a mighty world champion.
Paperback: £5.99

Killer
Charlie Seiga

His presence is a constant challenge to the lowlife who prey on those who can not defend themselves. His victims – liberty takers and sadists – are all hard bastards who deal in the most vicious violence. Charlie Seiga is a dangerous man. Men were murdered on Charlie's patch, and many times the police marked him out as the killer. But Charlie was the Houdini of the criminal world. Whenever he was arrested, he always had an alibi or a witness to say he wasn't guilty of the crime ...
Hardback: £15.99

Hard Bastards
Kate Kray

As seen on Channel 5's *Hard Bastards*.

Meet the hardest men in Britain. They fear no one. They live their life by the rules of the street and demand respect above all else. Kate Kray, widow of Ronnie Kray and top photographer Don Barrett, give a unique insight into thirty of the most feared and ruthless men in Britain.
Hardback: £14.99

Prices include post and packing in the UK.
Overseas and Eire, add £1.00 to the price of each book.

To order by credit card, telephone 020 7381 0666.

Or you can fill in the coupon over the page and send it with a cheque or postal order made payable to Blake Publishing Ltd, to:

Blake Publishing Ltd
Mail Order Department
3 Bramber Court, 2 Bramber Road
London
W14 9PB

Please send me a copy of each of the titles below:

❐	**The Guv'nor**	£14.99
❐	**Pretty Boy**	£14.99
❐	**Nosher**	£5.99
❐	**Bronson**	£14.99
❐	**Nigel Benn**	£5.99
❐	**Killer**	£15.99
❐	**Hard Bastards**	£14.99

Name   ....

Address   ....

....

....

Postcode   ....

Please allow 28 days for delivery.